HONEST
IMMIGRATION

HONEST IMMIGRATION.

HONEST IMMIGRATION.

www.honestimmigration.com

ISBN: 978-1-7341372-0-0 (print)
ISBN: 978-1-7341372-1-7(ebook)

Ordering Information:
Special discounts are available on quantity purchases by corporations, associations, and others. For details, contact www.honestimmigration.com

The following stories have been inspired by true events.

HONEST IMMIGRATION

How to Stay in the
United States Legally and
Become a Permanent Resident

ERIKA CISNEROS

HONEST IMMIGRATION.

CONTENTS

Chapter 1

Introduction

Your American Dream turned into an American Nightmare.

You came to the United States for happiness or work opportunities, or the chance to live in a safe and prosperous country.

Along the way, something went wrong.

Maybe you fell in love, but now your spouse or significant other no longer treats you well and you've been degraded and beaten. The emotional trauma is horrific. You feel as if there's nowhere to turn. No one can help you and you don't know what to do.

Maybe you came to America with an offer to work. But the job you voluntarily accepted turned out to be grueling, unsafe, degrading, or abusive. Perhaps someone you trusted took your passport. Or the pay you were supposed to receive never came. Perhaps you were constantly supervised and not allowed to talk to anyone. You couldn't leave—otherwise you were threatened with harm or with being reported to immigration. Perhaps you've escaped that situation or perhaps you are still there, wishing that someone would come and save you.

Maybe you were hurt by someone and you had to call the police to help you. Then, you reported everything you knew to the police so they could catch the aggressor. But afterward, you continued to suffer physically or emotionally.

Now, you wonder, "If I leave, where do I go?" "Will someone help me, or will I just be deported back to my home country?"

You Can Stay in the United States and Become a Resident

In the United States, there are three types of Humanitarian Visas that allow a person to stay if they have been mistreated, forced to work, or coerced to commit a commercial sex act: VAWA, U Visa and T Visa. Not everyone qualifies for these Humanitarian Visas; you must meet the requirements to get one.

The benefits of these Humanitarian Visas are: they lead to legal permanent residency, you can apply for the visa and residency *inside* of the United States, and you don't need anyone petitioning for you to apply.

As an attorney who has helped hundreds of violated immigrants throughout the United States apply for and secure Humanitarian Visas, I regularly encounter clients who don't think any of these laws could possibly apply to them. The visa process is complicated and there are many misconceptions about the United States immigration policy, so many people don't understand that it is possible to stay in America while pursuing a Humanitarian Visa.

The following are stories of individuals who thought they had no options. They lived hiding from immigration and were terrified of what would happen to them next.

When you read their stories, you will see many situations that men and women from different countries have experienced. Compare your situation and see which Humanitarian Visa was necessary to help them stay in the country legally. Realize that there are also other people who stayed in the country legally because of the injustice they suffered.

There will be an explanation of the requirements for each of the visas. In these stories, you may find a situation that is very close to your own. Discover the different options and know that there's a chance for justice and a better life.

Let us help you find justice. Contact us at www.honestimmigration.com.

Chapter 2

Luciana's Story

VAWA HELPS UNDOCUMENTED SPOUSES
OF UNITED STATES CITIZENS OR PERMANENT RESIDENTS
GAIN LEGAL STATUS ON THEIR OWN

Luciana gasped for air as Chris pinned her against the refrigerator and choked her with one hand. She couldn't move with the weight of his body pressing against hers. He tightened his hand around her neck as he held a knife to her head with his other hand. The lack of oxygen caused her vision to blur. She could feel herself losing consciousness.

She clawed at him, desperately pushing on his chest and trying to wiggle her way free, but she couldn't escape. She saw the rolling pin on the kitchen counter that she was using moments earlier to make Chris dinner.

She could see the children crying and scared in the living room after witnessing their father grab her by her hair and drag her around the kitchen floor. They had watched as he hit her head repeatedly against the floor with rage in his eyes. Then, he had lifted her up and slammed her against the refrigerator, shouting that he would teach her a lesson.

Terrified, they watched as she tried to fight off Chris. But he squeezed her neck tighter, still enraged.

She couldn't comfort them. She couldn't stop to hold them and tell them it was going to be okay. Would it be okay? Would their daddy kill her this time?

Chris had launched this assault after she interrupted his romantic phone call with another woman. Luciana was sick of being humiliated by Chris, who either treated her as if she didn't exist or was violent and abusive, and this time she had confronted him about his infidelity. He denied it all, but she knew he was lying like he had lied every other time before.

This time she had had enough. Enough of the years of abuse, the infidelity, and his frequent weekend disappearances. She thought about all the pain the children had endured over the years because of his selfishness.

The only escape from it all was to leave with the children. Her decision was written all over her face. Seeing her turn around and walk away from him made him furious and he lost control.

He threw his cell phone at her as she walked away from him to provoke her and gain control like he had done many times before. This was how he would change her mind. This was how he had always gotten his way. No matter what he did to her, he would either convince her to stay with his lies or force her to stay with his fists.

Luciana wasn't going to let him hurt her anymore. She wasn't going to waste another second of her life listening to the nonsense coming out of his mouth. She grabbed the cell phone and threw it back to him. She fought back for the very first time and told him he would never hurt her again. The anger and frustration she'd held inside for years was finally released.

In response, he attacked her.

Pinned against the refrigerator, she had one chance to escape his fatal grip, one chance to free herself before he used the knife on her. Her two babies…what would become of them if she didn't survive and they were forced to stay with this maniac who had never accepted them? He rejected his own blood, just like he rejected her, his high school sweetheart.

They had dated since high school. He was American and she was an immigrant from Venezuela living undocumented in the United States with her family. He was so loving and kind to her. He promised he would always love and protect her. She and her family thought he was the greatest blessing because he could provide her with a promising future.

Once they married, he could help her gain legal residency in the United States. She would have the chance to live the American Dream, which was the reason her parents had brought her to this country. Right after graduating high school, after she and Chris had dated for a couple years, Luciana became pregnant so they married sooner than expected.

Something changed after they married. He became cold, cruel, and abusive toward her. Later, he treated the children the same way. Despite all the infidelity, the humiliation, and watching helplessly as he beat their children, she stayed because she thought she could still love him. She hoped that the sweet boy she fell in love with would come back the next time he walked through her front door. However, the boy she once knew was never coming back.

She took the deepest breath she could and mustered what little strength she had left to reach for the rolling pin. Every second counted before she either lost consciousness or he killed her.

She swung as hard as she could and struck him on the head. The blow knocked him out instantly. She tried to catch her breath as his body went limp and he fell to the floor. Exhausted and shaking, she walked over his body where he'd fallen.

She immediately dialed 911. The 911 operator told her to find a safe place to wait for the police. Then, the police arrived and arrested Chris.

Luciana escaped with her children while Chris was in jail for domestic violence. She went to her family for help to leave Chris and move out of the house, which was in his name only. Luciana told her family how abusive he had been. Her family had not known how bad their marital problems had become; they had never suspected anything like this was going on with them. They had always loved Chris because they knew how much Luciana loved him.

Luciana's Problem

Luciana was finally able to escape her abusive United States citizen husband after several years of abuse. She was free from him, but she remained undocumented. Even though Chris was currently in jail, she still feared his threats of having her deported once he was released.

Luciana's story is common. We have all heard and read stories of women suffering from domestic violence. While statistics aren't conclusive regarding immigrants who are victims of domestic violence, Latino immigrants are far less likely to seek help when they are abused.

Domestic Violence Awareness Project. "What do we know about domestic violence within immigrant communities?"[1]

Women often don't escape from abusive relationships, even if their children are also suffering. Often they decide to stay, even though they continue to be mistreated.

Some would say that staying isn't a choice because no one chooses to be abused. The failure to leave could be considered more of a loss of hope, or fear of the unknown, and/or lack of confidence. Despite what you may call it, the result is the same: she stays and continues to be abused.

But what makes it different for those who choose not to continue in the cycle? Perhaps they don't make the decision to leave or to escape but simply make the decision that things will not continue to be the same.

---

1 https://nrcdv.org/dvam/sites/default/files2/Immigration%26DV-TalkingPointsForm.pdf.

Bad Advice

Prior to her final fight with her husband, Luciana had gone to see an immigration attorney to begin the family petition process so she could apply for residency based on her husband's United States citizenship. Luciana explained to the attorney that her husband was unwilling to assist with the process and that she would be doing it all on her own. However, because the attorney did not work on VAWA (Violence Against Women Act) cases, the attorney told Luciana that there was no way for her to gain residency unless it was with the help of her husband through the family petition process.

Furthermore, when Luciana mentioned that her husband was unwilling to help because they were having marital problems, the attorney asked Luciana if she had a police report proving that there had been domestic violence in the home. Unfortunately, the attorney did not know the VAWA requirements, which do not require a police report showing that there is domestic violence in the marriage. At that time in the marriage, Luciana had never reported the abuse to the police. It was the attorney's misinformation that made her believe that she could only apply for residency on her own if she had previously reported the abuse to the police.

Like so many other women before her, Luciana left the attorney's office defeated, believing that the only way for her to ever become a permanent resident was with the cooperation of her husband. During the point in the consultation when Luciana mentioned that her husband was unwilling to assist her with applying for residency, an attorney familiar with VAWA would have asked more probing questions to find out *why*. The key is finding out whether the husband is simply unwilling to help with the immigration process or whether the husband is abusive.

Luciana's bad experience with the attorney is quite common for people in her situation. The attorney Luciana consulted with was confusing the requirements for the U Visa with the requirements for VAWA. Although VAWA requires the applicant to have suffered battery/extreme cruelty by the United States citizen or permanent resident spouse, there is **_no_** police report required.

It wasn't until Luciana confided in a friend about the abuse she had suffered all those years living with Chris that her friend told her about the option to gain legal status for *undocumented* spouses of United States citizens or permanent residents.

Luciana did some research of her own on the internet and found that there did in fact exist an option called VAWA for undocumented abused women such as herself who had never become legal through their spouses.

Luciana finally called the office after months of living with the anxiety of the unknown, worrying whether she would in fact qualify or whether she would be rejected and told she couldn't do anything. She didn't know if she could bear any more pain after years of rejection and abuse from the man who was supposed to be her protector and who once was the love of her life.

How We Helped Luciana

When Luciana came to us, she was looking for hope. She wanted to find a way to gain legal status without Chris' help. Obviously, she didn't want anything to do with Chris.

During the consultation, she started off by letting us know that she was married to a United States citizen but he had never helped her gain legal status. That was an indication to us that she might be eligible for VAWA. Therefore, we asked her if she had lived with him at some point in the relationship in order to determine if she met the joint residence requirement for VAWA. She confirmed that she had.

However, it was the question about whether he had ever mistreated her that made her hesitate to answer. After a long pause, she said that he had yelled at her a few times and that their marriage had problems like all other marriages. We reassured her that the consultation we were having was private and that Chris would never know what she told us. We told her that she didn't have to go into the details of the mistreatment and instead she could just answer some yes or no questions.

As we asked her more general questions about the mistreatment, she felt comfortable simply answering yes or no. We asked her if Chris had ever been physically abusive and she said yes. We asked her if he had ever been verbally abusive and she said yes. We asked her if he had ever been sexually abusive toward her and forcing her to be intimate with him and she said yes.

After a few more questions, we asked her more specific questions regarding the different types of abuse. We asked her if he had ever slapped, kicked, or punched her. We asked her if he had ever cursed, insulted, or embarrassed her. We asked if he had ever been physically or verbally abusive while forcing her to be intimate with him. Again, she responded yes to most of the questions.

We told her we knew how difficult the relationship with Chris must have been. We also understood her not wanting to share the details of the abuse because of shame and embarrassment. We made sure she understood that we have worked with many clients in very similar situations and that we do not judge any of our clients. We assured her that we were there to help her move forward with her life.

Afterwards, we asked her if she could share with us the worst fight she could remember with Chris. Luciana sobbed and began to tell us about the incident that had landed Chris in jail.

We made her aware that VAWA was an option for her to gain legal status without Chris' help. We answered her questions and addressed her doubts and her fears. Luciana finally realized that she could gain legal status without the need to have Chris to petition for her. Chris did not need to be part of the process at all, and you can imagine what a relief that was for Luciana.

We then helped Luciana through each step of the process until a decision was made on her case. We kept in constant contact with her even when we were just waiting on a decision so as to ensure her that we were actively working on her case.

We started by helping Luciana gather the documents for her case, including her birth certificate and passport, and also her marriage certificate.

We also needed documentation or information proving that the abuser was a United States citizen or permanent resident, and the applicant has to show proof that they entered the marriage in good faith. In other words, that the marriage was entered into because the couple was in love and not just for the purpose of the undocumented spouse gaining permanent residency. This can be demonstrated with documents showing that the couple has had children together, that the couple shares or shared a residence, a bank account, or insurance, and/or has other bills in their names.

As with any immigration case, filing for VAWA is a lot of work. There is much that needs to be prepped, documented, and organized before submitting the VAWA case to immigration. It is extremely important that an applicant be cooperative with their attorney's office in getting all documents and information needed so that the office can complete the case and submit it. It is usually the applicant's cooperation that will determine how long the case will take to complete and be ready for submitting.

VAWA cases are filed with the Vermont Service Center (VSC), which is a department of immigration that handles all the filings of the Humanitarian Visas.

After an application is submitted, VSC issues a receipt notice to the applicant and the attorney notifying them that their case has been received and is now pending for processing.

Next, after the receipt notice is received, the applicant will receive a Prima Facie Approval letter or a Notice of Intent to Deny. A Prima Facie Approval letter allows the applicant to apply for some public assistance while their case is pending. A Notice of Intent to Deny is given when the VSC does not think that the case can be approved. At that time, the applicant is given more time to submit evidence that will change the VSC's opinion of the case.

Then, the applicant will receive their biometrics notice. This notifies the applicant that they have an appointment to go to the assigned immigration office to have their fingerprints taken.

After the fingerprints are taken, the applicant will receive a decision on their case. When they receive the decision depends on the processing times for VAWA cases at that time. Immigration processing times change constantly, and the current processing times can be found on the United States Citizenship and Immigration Services website.

Getting People to Understand They Are Victims Is the Hardest Part of the Process

Unfortunately, domestic violence victims like Luciana aren't in this situation because they are bad people. It's not because they don't care about their children enough. It's not because they are head over heels in love with the abuser. It's not because they are weak, or dumb, or cowards.

Many women and also men are sometimes forced to stay in awful situations. They may not be physically forced using chains, locks, or beatings. They may be forced with threats. Threats of hurting the victim or the children are common, or the abuser may even threaten to hurt themselves if the victim tries to leave.

It's rare to see a case where the domestic violence has gone on for only a short period of time. Typically, when the victim makes the decision to escape the situation, it's after years of trying to make things work, of hoping things will work out, and meanwhile suffering at the hands of the abuser.

Like Luciana, many victims don't seek help, especially when the victim is undocumented, and especially if the victim is somewhat isolated and not surrounded by family and/or friends. Sometimes, because of their undocumented status here in the United States, they don't realize that they can ask for help. They may believe that no law enforcement officer will believe them if they reach out for help. Others may think that even if they are believed, it will draw attention to their undocumented status and they will be deported. Typically, the fear of seeking help is related to their fear of their undocumented status being exposed.

Some victims will seek help with an immigration attorney because they understand that if they can just gain legal status, they can leave the abuser or at least seek the help they need from law enforcement and not have to worry about being deported.

However, a common mistake is that the victims don't tell the *truth* about the abuse when they do seek help from an immigration attorney. The victim will come to the attorney seeking help to become a permanent resident simply because they are married to a United States citizen or permanent resident. They falsely believe that the marriage alone can allow them to gain the legal status they so desperately need to escape the abuser.

Also, it is important to know that many attorneys do *not* focus on VAWA cases and don't understand the VAWA requirements. For that reason, many victims are given the wrong advice. They may be told that they are unable to gain legal status without the help of their legal spouse. Then, the victim will leave the attorney's office brokenhearted and hopeless.

Therefore, it is important for the person who needs help to speak to an attorney who is well versed in VAWA cases. The attorney will know what questions to ask to determine if the person qualifies for VAWA. These questions must be asked because most victims will not mention the abuse—because they believe that speaking of the abuse will hurt their chances of being able to become a permanent resident. They don't know that this is not true.

Like Luciana, if they *do* speak of the abuse, they may not talk about the *extent* of the abuse. They may just say that they have *normal* problems in their marriage. However, normal can mean a lot of things. Some victims have considered being slapped frequently and/or chased with a knife as *normal*. Others have considered being forced to cook at 3:00 a.m. for their drunk spouse *normal*. Although there may be no physical abuse involved, *forcing* someone to do something is still abuse.

This is the point in the conversation where an attorney who understands VAWA will begin to ask the subtle questions to get the victim to speak about the abuse. The first piece of advice regarding getting the victim to talk about the abuse is to not refer to it as *abuse*. Instead, it should be referred to as *problems* or *trouble* in the marriage.

Victims who don't speak of the abuse typically aren't doing it to protect the abuser. They aren't doing it because they don't want to give the abuser a bad rap. The victim usually hides the abuse because they are *embarrassed*. Many times, they come from a culture where the marriage is seen as sacred and anything that happens in it, including abuse, is not to be discussed with anyone other than their spouse. Other cultures give women a lowly place where they are to expect whatever treatment they get from their husbands and see it as normal.

When I've had a client that does not want to open up about the abuse but continues to refer to the marriage as "troublesome," I use examples. Sometimes examples help the victim to understand that these things happen to others as well. The examples also help them to understand what is considered abuse. The victim may not know that a specific incident is considered abuse.

Abuse that is not physical is much more difficult for victims to see as *abuse*. The victim knows that it's not right or that they are hurt, humiliated, or embarrassed by it, but they don't know that it's *abuse*. This happens with economic abuse or isolation or threats. Victims will dismiss economic abuse, especially if they are a stay-at-home spouse. They feel no right to the finances since they do not work outside of the home. Isolation is often dismissed as jealousy, and threats can also be dismissed.

Like Luciana, many victims will talk themselves out of the option to gain residency. They believe rumors from other people that have misinformed them regarding what will limit their options to apply for residency. Luciana believed she could not qualify for anything because she had entered the United States undocumented. She also believed that the only way she could ever apply for residency was if her husband applied for her. Both beliefs were incorrect.

Chapter 3

Everything You Need
to Know About VAWA

VAWA HELPS SPOUSES, PARENTS, AND CHILDREN
OBTAIN RESIDENCY WHEN NO ONE WANTS
TO HELP THEM GAIN LEGAL STATUS

Many applicants scare themselves out of wanting to apply for VAWA even after they discover that it is an option that exists. They fear that the abuser will find out they are applying under VAWA. They fear that the abuser will be harmed if they apply. They fear that they must leave the country for an interview with immigration. They fear that just by applying, immigration will find out that they are living undocumented in the United States and will come and deport them.

Will the abuser find out about the VAWA application?

The only way that an abuser can find out about the application is if the VAWA Self-Petitioner tells the abuser about applying. The attorney representing the VAWA Self-Petitioner is under a legal obligation under the attorney-client privilege to keep all information between attorney and client private. The client is allowed to share with others any information they choose, but the attorney is legally not allowed to do so. Furthermore, immigration does not notify or verify for the abuser whether the VAWA Self-Petitioner has applied

17

for VAWA. Immigration does this to protect the VAWA Self-Petitioner because there is no way to know what the abuser would do to the VAWA Self-Petitioner upon finding out.

Will the abuser be harmed because the VAWA Self-Petitioner applies for VAWA?

Many times, VAWA Self-Petitioners worry that if they apply for VAWA, the abuser will somehow be negatively affected. Their worry may result from the fact that the VAWA Self-Petitioner and the abuser have children together. However, the abuser is not affected in any way. Therefore, if a background check was to be done on the abuser, the VAWA Self-Petitioner's VAWA filing would not appear. The VAWA application does not prevent the abuser from being able to apply for a job, or attend a college, or gain custody of their children.

VAWA Self-Petitioners sometimes believe that if they file for VAWA, the abuser will be arrested or at least interrogated by the police. However, this is not true. The police do not get involved in any way just because the VAWA Self-Petitioner has applied for VAWA.

Must the applicant travel outside of the United States to an interview for VAWA?

VAWA Self-Petitioners do not have to travel outside of the United States for any part of the VAWA Self-Petition. The application is completed while living in the United States. The biometrics appointment for fingerprints is done inside of the United States. When the VAWA Self-Petition is granted, it is mailed to the VAWA Self-Petitioner inside of the United States. Unlike a family petition process where a family member is petitioning for the beneficiary, with a VAWA Self-Petition there is no consular interview in the applicant's home country.

Will immigration find out that the applicant is living in the United States undocumented and come to deport them?

One of the biggest concerns for people that are living undocumented in the United States is that immigration will find out that they are here undocumented. Therefore, they believe that by not filing an application with immigration it will help them remain hidden from immigration and safe from the risk of being deported.

However, remaining *undocumented* keeps the person at risk of being deported at any given moment. Every day that a person is living undocumented in the United States, they are at risk of being deported. Not because the person may have done something terrible or criminally felonious to cause the deportation but merely by the fact that the person is undocumented is a reason to be at risk of deportation.

Immigration already knows that there are millions of people living undocumented in the United States. They discover this many ways. There are many undocumented children enrolled in the school system that most likely have parents who are undocumented as well. There are people who file their income taxes using ITIN numbers that have residences within the United States. There are undocumented people birthing children in the hospitals every year that are listed on the child's birth certificates as being born outside the United States. Many police departments have records of undocumented people that have been pulled over for not having a driver's license. Many undocumented people have either personally applied for government benefits or applied for benefits on behalf of their children. The point is that there are many ways that immigration can find out who is undocumented and where they live.

Another easy way that immigration finds people living undocumented is to just show up at jobsites or in cities or set up checkpoints on roadways. It is not difficult for immigration to find someone who is undocumented.

The reason that there are so many undocumented people that continue to live in the United States is because immigration does not have the resources or the manpower to track down and detain every single undocumented person. What people don't understand is how costly it is to track a person down.

Why is applying to gain legal status the best option?

The best thing that an undocumented person can do is to find a way to gain legal status in the United States. This starts with the simple first step of seeking legal advice from a licensed immigration attorney. Upon finding out that there is an option, the person should continue with applying for that option. There is no benefit in having an option but not applying for it. *If a person is detained, the immigration court wants to know if the person is applying for an immigration process that will allow them to stay legally in the United States.* Otherwise, in most cases, the immigration court will order the undocumented person deported because there would be no point in having an immigration court if the undocumented person could just stay without having to gain legal status.

VAWA Qualification Requirements

While VAWA stands for Violence Against Women Act, it can be obtained by both men and women. The person applying for VAWA is called the VAWA Self-Petitioner.

To qualify for VAWA, the VAWA Self- Petitioner must meet the following basic requirements.

First, the VAWA Self- Petitioner must be a battered child, parent, or spouse.

A battered child must be under the age of 21 years old and unmarried and abused by a United States citizen or permanent resident. The VAWA Self-Petitioner can also file for VAWA after the age of 21, but before the age of 25, if it can be proven that the abuse was the cause for the delay in filing.

A battered parent must be the parent of a United States citizen son or daughter that is at least the age of 21 years old at the time of applying for VAWA. The parent of a permanent resident would not be able to apply.

For battered spouses, the undocumented VAWA Self-Petitioner must either be currently married to, or recently divorced from, a United States citizen or permanent resident.

If the couple is living separately, then the couple is still considered to be married. Even if the couple has been living separately for years or even decades, they are still married so long as neither the VAWA Self- Petitioner nor their spouse has filed for and has been granted a divorce.

One question I often get asked by VAWA Self-Petitioners who have been separated for many years and sometimes even over a decade is, "How do I know if I'm still married to my spouse?" It's important to know that no law exists that will automatically divorce couples who have been separated for extended amounts of time. Therefore, divorce would require that one of the spouses file for divorce and then have it granted to them and ordered by a judge. The simplest way for the VAWA Self-Petitioner to find out if there has been a divorce is to ask the United States citizen or permanent resident spouse if they have ever filed for and been granted a divorce. However, if there is no communication between the spouses, then finding out if there is a divorce can be impossible. The reason it can be difficult to figure out is because a United States citizen or permanent resident spouse could have gotten divorced anywhere in the country. It is not required to get divorced in the same city or state where you were married. So that would mean having to check every city and state in the country to find out if a divorce was granted.

Many people think that their spouse cannot get divorced without their permission and signature. So they assume that because they have not signed for a divorce, they cannot be divorced. However, many courts will grant a divorce to a person without their spouse's knowledge. Even if there are mutual children, a judge may grant the divorce. Granting the divorce is not the same as deciding the custody of the children. The custody of the children is some-thing that a judge can only decide with both spouses' permission. Therefore, if a couple has mutual children, one spouse can be granted a divorce without the other spouse's permission. But the custody of the children will remain undetermined.

If the couple is divorced, the divorce must be no more than two years old. Under VAWA, a VAWA Self-Petitioner that has been divorced from a United States citizen or permanent resident spouse for over two years will no longer qualify for VAWA. The date that will determine the two-year mark of the divorce is the date on the judge's order granting the divorce. This date should not be confused with the date of the filing of the divorce.

If either spouse has filed for and been granted a divorce, the VAWA Self-Petitioner should not marry anyone else until after getting a decision on their VAWA case. Marrying will automatically end their opportunity to obtain a visa under VAWA. This rule does not indicate that the VAWA Self-Petitioner will never be able to marry again. It simply means that the marriage must take place after the VAWA case has been decided; otherwise it will disqualify the VAWA Self- Petitioner from obtaining a visa under VAWA.

If the United States citizen or permanent resident spouse is deceased, the rule is the same as if there had been a divorce. The VAWA Self-Petitioner must file for VAWA within two years of the United States citizen or permanent resident spouse's death. Similarly, the VAWA Self-Petitioner cannot marry anyone until the VAWA case has been decided by immigration. Marriage would disqualify the VAWA Self-Petitioner from qualifying for a visa under VAWA.

Second, the VAWA Self-Petitioner and the abuser must have resided together.

A battered child must have resided with the abusive parent.

A battered parent must have resided with the abusive United States citizen son or daughter.

For battered spouses, the United States citizen or permanent resident spouse must have lived together.

There is no limit on the amount of time that the VAWA Self-Petitioner had to live with the abuser. The important thing is that they lived to together at some point.

The VAWA Self-Petitioner must provide proof of joint residency.

For a child or a parent, the proof of joint residency can be in the form of school records, medical records, or records from a department of child and family services.

For spouses, this can include proof in the form of a utility bill, a lease, or any other piece of mail showing that the couple lived at the same address.

Third, the VAWA Self-Petitioner must have suffered battery/extreme cruelty by the United States citizen or permanent resident parent, spouse, son, or daughter.

Abuse and Mistreatment Can Come in Many Different Forms

Abuse can occur in many forms. The most common is physical abuse. Physical abuse can include biting, scratching, and pulling hair in addition to slapping, punching, and kicking.

If the person is not being *physically* abused, it can sometimes be confusing as to whether or not they can meet this third requirement. This is especially true for men who are the victims in the relationship. Many men don't even consider physical abuse as mistreatment. They will in fact consider the abuse normal just because they are a man.

There are also other types of abuse that are very common but not recognized as abuse in the relationship. Below, we discuss these different types of abuse and show how they manifest in a relationship.

EMOTIONAL ABUSE: This type of abuse is very common. It can include cursing, yelling, humiliation, false accusations, and controlling behavior. Sometimes the abuser will use racist names to address the victim. The abuser may humiliate the victim in front of the children, or in front of family and friends, by using racist names or calling out the victim's undocumented immigration status. Constant accusations of being unfaithful also fall under this category, as well as controlling the way the victim dresses. Complete control over any area of the victim's life is emotional abuse.

ECONOMIC ABUSE: This can be tricky because in a home where there is economic abuse there is usually only one spouse financially supporting the family. However, many times it is the abuser that takes full control of the finances, and the victim is left without any access to the finances. Other times, the victim is left paying all the living expenses and it is the abuser that spends the finances carelessly to the point where there isn't enough for household necessities.

SEXUAL ABUSE: This too can be a gray area because victims fail to understand that they have the right to refuse to have sexual intercourse with their spouse. The victim is usually physically forced to have intercourse. During intercourse, the abuser may also be physically abusive or make the victim do things that are uncomfortable, degrading, or painful.

USING THE CHILDREN: Many abusers will use the children to control and manipulate. The abuser may use the children to keep the victim in the relationship. At times, the abuser will threaten to leave and take the children so the victim will never see them again. Other times, the abuser will turn the children against the victim.

THREATS: Threats are very common in abusive relationships. The threat of deportation is frequently used in relationships where there is an undocumented spouse. The abuser may openly threaten to have the victim deported or may be subtler by threatening to call the police. In some situations, if the abuser has already started the immigration process to help the victim gain Legal Permanent Residency, the abuser may threaten to withdraw the application.

USING THEIR UNITED STATES CITIZEN OR PERMANENT RESIDENT STATUS: The abuser may use his United States citizen or permanent resident status to convince the victim that no legal authority would believe the victim over the abuser because of the abuser's legal status. The abuser may also use his/her legal status to convince the victim that they have the right to make all decisions regarding the children.

INTIMIDATION: For example, the abuser can destroy or threaten to destroy the victim's important documents such as a passport, an ID card, or other documents that come from the victim's home country.

ISOLATION: The isolation may begin gradually as the abuser limits the victim's contact with others. It may begin with limiting the victim's time calling or visiting friends. Then, it may move on to include limited time with family. Other times, the abuser demands that the victim not call or visit any family or friends.

What if I Was Never Physically Abused?

This is one of the most common questions that I hear. Usually the victim claims that they were never physically abused, which is true in rare instances. However, it is usually the case that there had been some physical abuse in the relationship but the victim has dismissed it by considering the treatment "normal."

Victims have referred to being slapped, being scratched, having their arm or hair pulled, being tripped, or getting pinched as "normal" physical abuse in the relationship. This abuse may seem insignificant to the victim because it has only happened occasionally or it did not cause severe harm. Other times, this type of abuse is culturally accepted in a relationship. Furthermore, the victim's culture may prohibit the spouse speaking of the physical abuse.

I Don't Have a Police Report, so How Will Immigration Believe Me?

VAWA does *not* require a police report. This has been a wide misconception since the *U Visa*—which is set aside for people who are victims of criminal activity and are willing to aid authorities—*does* require the victim to show he/she has been helpful, will be helpful, or will likely be helpful to law enforcement in investigating and prosecuting the crime. The easiest way to show this is by providing a police report that shows that the victim has aided law enforcement by reporting the crime. Unfortunately, many attorneys that are not up to date on VAWA give incorrect information regarding the proof that is required for VAWA.

The fact that a police report is not required does not mean that no proof is necessary. The applicant must include, as part of their signed VAWA Self-Petition, written testimony that describes in detail the abuse they suffered.

Today, we have forgotten the value of our word. Therefore, applicants don't understand why anyone would believe them without a police report or third-party account of the abuse. Applicants don't believe their word has any value. Thus, they believe they need evidence to give their word credibility.

However, immigration is still very old fashioned in a sense and does value and give credibility to an applicant's testimony. The credibility comes from the detail in the applicant's personal declaration describing the abuse. The applicant's signature on the personal declaration further establishes truth.

Marrying a Resident or a United States Citizen Is Never an Automatic Route to Gain Legal Status

People who are unfamiliar with the immigration process assume that becoming a permanent resident is quick and easy after marrying someone who is a United States citizen or permanent resident. Little do they know that the costly process can take several years and is very risky because it usually requires having to leave the United States to do an interview at the United States Consulate in the beneficiary's home country.

Why is that risky? Well, because there is no guarantee that the beneficiary will be approved for residency and will be able to return to the United States. If the beneficiary is denied residency, then the beneficiary is stuck in their home country and unable to return to the United States. Having United States citizen children, having an established United States business, having lived in the United States for over a decade, or even the fact that your family can't speak the beneficiary's home country's language will not make a difference. The beneficiary is stuck with no option to return to the United States. A family can be torn apart in an instant.

It is also believed that marrying someone who is a United States citizen or permanent resident will automatically give the spouse residency. On the other hand, there are people who believe that residency is not automatic but that it is guaranteed to the spouse upon applying. Both beliefs are wrong. Residency is not automatic and it is certainly not guaranteed to the spouse of a United States citizen or permanent resident.

Unfortunately, it is common for the spouse of a United States citizen or permanent resident not to be able to gain residency through the marriage. This has nothing to do with the undocumented spouse committing a felonious crime. It does, however, have everything to do with antiquated immigration laws that keep these spouses from gaining residency due to their undocumented entries into the United States.

Usually, an undocumented spouse cannot gain residency because of a law that is known as the "10-year bar" or the "permanent bar." This "10-year bar" prohibits the undocumented spouse from gaining residency if they accrued more than one year of unlawful presence in the United States. The "permanent bar" prohibits the undocumented spouse from gaining residency if they accrued more than one year of unlawful presence in the United States, left the United States, and then returned to the United States undocumented. To remove the bars, the undocumented spouse must wait outside of the United States for 10 years before beginning the residency process.

It is common for someone who has been in the United States for more than a few years to be under the permanent bar because they have been in the United States for more than one year undocumented, they have exited the United States, and then returned to the United States undocumented. People leave the United States for many different reasons, most commonly to visit family, to visit terminally ill family members, or to attend family funerals.

Although there is a way around these bars, which is living outside of the United States for 10 years, it is not realistically feasible. Most people, and especially most couples, cannot live outside of the United States for a decade. Not only is the exaggerated time limit a problem but many of the people have commitments in the United States such as careers, children, and family. Others may find the move impossible because they don't know the language or the culture since they have lived in the United States the majority of their lives.

WHAT HAPPENS AFTER I APPLY FOR VAWA?

✓ **30 DAYS AFTER SUBMITTING YOUR APPLICATION TO IMMIGRATION,** YOU WILL RECEIVE A RECEIPT INDICATING THAT YOUR CASE IS PENDING.

✓ **120 DAYS AFTER SUBMITTING YOUR APPLICATION TO IMMIGRATION,** YOU WILL RECEIVE YOUR BIOMETRICS APPOINTMENT.

✓ **60 - 90 DAYS AFTER SUBMITTING YOUR APPLICATION TO IMMIGRATION,** YOU WILL RECEIVE ANOTHER NOTIFICATION.

✓ **YOUR CASE WILL BE PROCESSED ACCORDING TO THE PROCESSING TIMES LISTED ON THE USCIS.GOV WEBSITE,** THEN YOU WILL RECEIVE A DECISION ON YOUR CASE.

Processing times are approximate.

HONEST IMMIGRATION.

Chapter 4

Natalia's Story

Natalia was born in Honduras, and she was married to Ivan, who is a United States citizen. They met in Chicago, Illinois. At the time, she lived in a house with her cousin. Ivan was the sweetest man she had ever met and she was in love with him. He treated her like a princess.

Even though they were just dating, Ivan always made sure she had what she needed. She felt that she had found her Prince Charming.

One evening, while they were out with some friends for dinner, he proposed. She was ecstatic. To honor tradition, Ivan had previously called and asked her father in Honduras for her hand in marriage. Their families were happy. They had a small intimate wedding with his family, her cousin and a few close friends.

Right after the honeymoon, they moved into a house in Chicago with two of his cousins and their wives, and they lived together for five years.

The Beginning of Violence

Immediately after they married, Ivan began to change. Anything would cause him to become frustrated and lose his temper. It didn't bother her too much that he was always having mood swings, until one day it went from bad to worse.

They went out to dinner one night. When they got to the restaurant, she got out of the car and left her jacket in the car. She was wearing a tank top. Ivan got angry with her when he noticed that she had taken her jacket off. He pushed her back toward the car. He demanded that she go back to the car and put on her jacket.

She had no clue why he was so angry; everything had been fine just moments earlier. She explained that she had just forgotten the jacket. Ivan became furious. He went inside the restaurant with everyone else and made her stay in the car. He threatened he would make a scene if she came inside. It was freezing without the heater on, so she called everyone's cell phone to get them to calm Ivan down, but no one answered to help her.

It wasn't long before Ivan was criticizing everything about her—her clothes, her cooking, her way of speaking, her mannerisms, her weight. He would find the smallest thing to scream about and nothing was good enough for him. She felt emotional pain as he compared her to other women and his cousins' wives. He said he hated everything about her and that he wished they had never married.

Ivan would pick her clothes out for her because if she dressed herself, he would make her change until he was satisfied with what she was wearing. At times, he was so disgusted with her that he would throw her clothes in the garbage and spill grease on them so she couldn't get them out of the trash.

Family Humiliation

She hated weekends because his friends would usually come over. His cousins would invite their friends as well. Then, Ivan would act like a circus leader and she was treated like the clown. He made jokes and everyone laughed. She was embarrassed and humiliated. Even then, his family didn't realize how hurtful he was being, or they just didn't care. She felt worthless and unwanted, and she couldn't figure out how Ivan had gone from being the man of her dreams to someone who made her feel as if she was living in hell on earth.

It wasn't long before she had no friends at all. When her friends invited her out, Ivan wouldn't let her go. Any time a friend called, Ivan made her hang up. He also prohibited her from seeing her cousin, who was the only relative she had in town.

Forced to Stop Working

Ivan forced her to quit her job because he said that if she didn't quit he would find a way to get her fired. She couldn't leave the house without him, and he sold her car so she couldn't drive anywhere. She was completely dependent on him for everything, which is just what he wanted—to be able to control her.

Once he forced her to stop working and driving, she went without a lot of things that she had become accustomed to. She didn't have a single penny to her name. Ivan wouldn't give her any money and she didn't know what he did with his money.

The financial situation got a lot worse once their first child was born. There were so many things that she needed for the baby, but Ivan refused to buy them. She was not allowed to buy disposable diapers because he said he was raised on cloth diapers. Without her income, they were barely able to make ends meet.

Ivan Stabbed at Work

One day, Ivan was the victim of an armed robbery at work. He was stabbed multiple times and his cousin, who was almost killed in the attack, was left paralyzed from the neck down.

Natalia hated what had happened to Ivan and his cousin, but she thought that Ivan might change. It could be a wakeup call for him to appreciate what he had in his life. She decided to forgive Ivan for how he had treated her in the past, for their family's sake. This was her chance to show Ivan how much she loved him and things would go back to being as they were when they dated.

Ivan had been stabbed in the abdomen, so she made special liquid meals for him so he could digest the food. She went to great lengths to make him the best meals possible and she checked on him frequently to make sure he was always comfortable. Things were great for a few days until the medicine wore off and Ivan started to stay awake for longer periods of time.

Ivan's Abuse Gets Worse

Ivan started treating her even worse than before the robbery. One evening, Ivan decided he wanted to come to the table to have dinner with his family. Everyone was happy he felt well enough to come and eat at the table again. She made his favorite dish in liquid form to celebrate his improvement, and she placed it in front of him hoping that this would make him happy. Without saying a word, he threw the hot liquid in her face. It burned horribly and she couldn't get it off fast enough. Afterwards, her face blistered. It was the most painful and humiliating thing she had ever experienced.

All Alone but Surrounded by Family

All his family around the table watched the whole thing in shock. But not one of them defended her or bothered to get the hot liquid off her face or asked if she was okay.

It was on this day she realized that even though she lived with his family members, she was alone. No one was going to do anything to help her escape the misery. They were his family, not hers. This made her even more fearful because to them it was acceptable for Ivan to hurt her. They would simply carry on as if nothing had happened.

His Drinking Begins

Once Ivan healed and returned to work, he started to drink alcohol, and not just on the weekends. Every afternoon, he drank until he got drunk and angry, and he constantly insulted her. It was as if he blamed Natalia for everything that he was disappointed with in his life.

When he screamed at her, she could feel the hate, and she realized that there was nothing she could say or do to change things. At times, he would say he was so disgusted with her that he couldn't bear to look at her for a second longer, and he would kick her out of the house.

Violence Toward Her Friend

One day, a friend whom Natalia had not seen in a very long time found out where she lived and came over to visit. As they sat in the living room catching up, Ivan came home. In front of her friend, he demanded that Natalia go into their bedroom and have sex with him. Natalia was so humiliated and embarrassed.

The friend didn't know what to say or do and she felt terrible for not being able to help. Then, when Natalia didn't move fast enough, he started trying to take her clothes off in front of her friend. Natalia pushed him away, but he pulled her into the bedroom, slammed her onto the bed, and forced her to have sex with him. When it was over, she got up and walked out to the living room, thankful that her friend had left.

Natalia became pregnant again, and she clung to the hope that this would be the reason for Ivan to change. The news of her pregnancy infuriated Ivan. He called her every name in the book and made her sleep in the living room from that day on.

He rarely acknowledged her, but as her belly began to grow, he began referring to her as a fat animal. He made sure to insult her until she cried every day.

Kicked Out of the Home

Natalia never went to the police to report Ivan's abusive behavior toward her or the children because she was undocumented and she feared being deported. More than just fearing being deported, Natalia feared leaving her children behind with their ruthless father. She feared they would not be taken care of properly if she was not around to care for them. She also feared never being able to see them again upon returning to the United States. She didn't know if Ivan would keep them from her or move away so she couldn't find them.

In his fits of rage, he would kick her out and she would have to leave immediately. He would let her take the children but not gather any of their things. They had to leave with whatever clothing they were wearing. Knowing that they might be ejected from their home at any moment, she always made sure they were fully dressed and wearing shoes. Her existence became a living hell.

Natalia confided in her cousin about the abuse, so she would let her stay in her home if she needed to. Natalia would be forced to leave all their belongings with him. It was another way of his showing her that he was in control. But every time Ivan kicked her out of the house, he would come looking for her the next day. He would pound on her cousin's door, yelling and begging for forgiveness. Embarrassed, her cousin would usually ask her to go back because she feared that he would cause trouble for her as well.

Ivan's Hollow Promises

Sometimes, Ivan would promise to change and say that things were going to be like they had been early on. Natalia always felt that she had no choice except to go back. She had no money and two children, and there was no one who could help her financially.

After she'd return, he would behave for a couple of days, then pick up where he had left off. Then, before long, he would threaten her and kick her out of the house again.

The Escape

One day there were policemen that came knocking on the door and Natalia answered. They asked for Ivan, but she told them that he was at work. The police told her they were searching for him because he had been stalking a young girl.

That night, Ivan didn't come home, and his cousins didn't say anything about his whereabouts. A week later, Ivan still hadn't come home and no one was giving her any updates. Finally, a couple of weeks later, Natalia overheard them talking and found out that Ivan had been arrested. They mentioned that he was going to be sentenced to several years in jail.

Natalia saw this as her opportunity to escape. She contacted one of her friends whom she had also told about the abuse. At first, the friend was hesitant to help Natalia, but she agreed once she knew that Ivan was in jail and couldn't cause trouble. Natalia and the children moved in with her friend, and she found a job. She stayed there until she had saved enough money to move out of the state. To this day, Natalia has not seen Ivan nor heard any news about him. She believes he is still in jail.

Seeking Help as Soon as Possible

Natalia should have called the police long before Ivan kicked her out of the home. Calling the police after Ivan kicked her out of the home with the children would have likely led to receiving help from law enforcement to find a battered women's shelter that would keep her from having to return to Ivan. In domestic violence situations, especially if there are children involved, the focus is on getting help for the victim, and it is also vital to keep the children away from the abusive situation. Most shelters for battered women not only help undocumented women find help to keep them away from the abusive relationship, they also have someone who will help them gain legal immigration status. The assistance is provided to help the undocumented victim be able to make a life for herself and for her children.

Sexual Abuse Can Exist in a Marriage

Just because you are married does not mean you have to perform sexually in a way that is abhorrent to you.

Throughout their marriage, Ivan would force Natalia to have oral sex. He knew that she didn't feel comfortable with it but she didn't have any choice. If she didn't want to perform oral sex on him, he would grab her by the hair and force her to do it.

She would plead with him not to make her do it but that just made him angrier and more aggressive. Their sex life was not romantic and intimate; it was dirty and painful. She was disgusted by it and it hurt her both physically and emotionally.

Ivan's response to her cries and pleas was that she was his wife and she had a duty to please him. It wasn't uncommon for her to have bruises all over her body after sex. He made her wear clothing and makeup that would cover up the bruising. He told her never to disclose anything about their sex life and he threatened her.

However, Natalia did not owe any sexual duty to Ivan just because she was married to him. Natalia had every right to make decisions about her own body. Ivan did not own her body just because he was her husband. Natalia did not have to perform sexual acts against her will or acts that she was uncomfortable performing.

In many cultures, women are not taught that they have a choice when it comes to being intimate with their husband. They are made to believe that their husband has the right to use their body for sex whenever and however the husband chooses. It is much less common for women to be told how their husbands should treat them during intimacy. No one teaches women the difference between intimacy and sexual abuse. It is for this reason that women do not know they are being sexually abused.

Although sexual abuse exists in marriages, many women do not even identify themselves as victims of sexual abuse. These women do not understand that there are boundaries during intimacy as well. Abuse and pain and disrespect do not have to be accepted.

Rape also exists in marriages, but again, women do not identify themselves as rape victims. These women do not know that they can refuse to have sex with their husband. They also don't know that they are rape victims when they are being forced by their husband to have sex.

How We Helped Natalia

When Natalia came to us, she had lived under Ivan's control and abuse for years. She should have looked for help much sooner. However, like Natalia, many women do not look for help because they are afraid, or because they don't know how to ask for help, or *who* to ask for help.

We helped Natalia feel comfortable sharing her story with us. When the abuser is the spouse, asking for help can be embarrassing. The victim has to tell someone that they are victims in their own marriage. And this requires giving details about the abuse that will likely be uncomfortable and embarrassing to talk about.

We explained to Natalia the many types of problems that can exist in a marriage so as to help her feel at ease sharing about the abuse she had suffered. For many sexually abused women, there exists the fear that no one will believe their story. Rape, after all, is something that usually happens between strangers, not spouses, or at least that's what many people believe. Not knowing how someone will react when you tell them that your husband rapes you can create fear, so much so that the victim will choose to remain silent.

Initially, Natalia did not volunteer the information about how Ivan sexually abused her. Normally, victims of sexual abuse must be asked whether there was any abuse in the bedroom. Victims will usually answer that their spouse made them have sex even though they did not want to, but they will not come out and openly say their spouse raped them.

We assured Natalia that we were there to help her, just as we have helped many others in similar situations. Like Natalia, many victims don't know how to ask for help or who to ask for help. Natalia knew that Ivan's family saw the abuse, but they refused to assist her in any way. This gave Natalia the false belief that no one would help her escape from Ivan. It also gave Natalia the false belief that she had to put up with the abuse because Ivan was her husband.

We helped Natalia to visualize a life that didn't include Ivan. Sometimes victims will go to family or friends for help first. However, that can be a bad idea if they don't know how to help the victim; or worse, they encourage the victim to stay in the abusive marital relationship and work things out with their spouse. This can give the victim the impression that it is up to them to do better or to change to make the spouse stop the abuse.

Chapter 5

Franco's Story

VAWA HELPS MEN GAIN LEGAL STATUS
WHEN THEIR WIVES DON'T WANT TO HELP THEM

Franco was born in Guatemala. He came to the United States in 2003 and got married to a United States citizen, Nicole.

Franco and Nicole met through a cousin that was dating her friend. They began dating, having fun, and frequently going out to dinner and the movies. And they often went out as a group with Nicole's two daughters from a previous relationship.

Franco loved being with Nicole and loved her daughters like his own children. They dated for about a year, then moved together into his apartment, where he lived with his roommate and his roommate's girlfriend. They decided to get married.

The Trouble Begins

Franco loved Nicole but they had issues even before they got married. They were hanging out with her family, and he was watching a football game with her brother. Nicole asked him to go with her to the kitchen, and when he refused, she grabbed the lamp on the end table and struck him with it multiple times, breaking the lamp. Nicole's brother called 911 because he thought

Franco was dead. Franco didn't press charges, which is often the case with men who are assaulted by their girlfriend or wife.

After they got married, Nicole seemed to go back to normal. But then she began to change.

First, Nicole started to act differently around him, and then she became very jealous and possessive. She didn't want him leaving the house without her, and if he did, she would get very angry.

Over time, her controlling behavior became worse. The only place he was allowed to go without her was to his workplace. He couldn't come home late or she would accuse him of having an affair, and it got to the point where he couldn't talk to anyone.

When he was home, she wouldn't let him walk outside in the yard. She wouldn't let him look out the window because she believed he was staring at women, and eventually, she painted the windows with black paint.

Franco wanted to leave, but Nicole had threatened to do something horrible to him or get him deported if he left.

Sometimes when Franco got home from work, she would make him go straight to the bedroom. If he didn't comply, she would get physically aggressive.

At dinnertime, he would only eat if she made enough food for both of them to eat. He was not allowed to get any food from the kitchen or the refrigerator.

Lies She Told

Before their marriage, they had talked about Nicole starting the immigration process so he could become a United States permanent resident with her help. When they began that process, the abuse got worse.

Franco would come home from work and Nicole would be high on drugs. She would accuse him of being with her only to get residency. She would accuse him of being unfaithful and claimed that he would leave her for another woman. She would become angry when Franco would contact the attorney's office on his own about his immigration process.

At that point, Nicole became even stricter and wouldn't allow him to talk to his family. Franco felt like he lived in hell.

Nicole's anger turned into screams, insults, and physical abuse. She would slap him until she felt satisfied. And she would kick him, pinch him, and pull his hair.

Franco was a lost soul and he took whatever she dished out.

Sexual Abuse

Because of the way he was being treated, he didn't want to be intimate anymore. He was scared to be near her. But because he didn't want to be intimate with her, she assumed that it was because he had been cheating on her. This would make her even angrier. She would push him onto the bed and demand sex. If he said no, she would start punching and slapping him until he followed her directions. If he were to defend himself with physical violence, he feared that she would call the police and he'd be thrown in jail or deported.

She would force him to have sex daily and would fight him if he didn't have sex with her, thus causing him to be late for work. Eventually, his tardiness caused him to lose his job—and he was the sole financial provider for the family.

Humiliation Around Others

Around other people, she would constantly embarrass Franco. He avoided social gatherings with her family and friends because she would scream and humiliate him in front of them. There were times in public when she would hit him, curse at him, and make a scene. If someone called him on his cell phone, he would have an anxiety attack because of what Nicole might do.

Nicole also made sure that Franco never received any information from their immigration attorney's office because she called and told them lies about him.

The Final Straw and Humiliation

After Franco lost his job, they moved into her parent's home, and it immediately became a jail cell for Franco. Nicole turned her parents and her siblings who lived there into his prison guards. She gave orders that he should not leave their bedroom and made them give her a detailed account of everything he did while she was out. Every night, she would leave the house and leave her daughters with him. She'd go out to party with friends and get high. Many nights, she didn't come home at all.

The worse incident occurred when all four of them were in the car. Nicole became angry with Franco while she was driving. She went crazy and purposely drove them into the ditch. No one was injured but that was the final straw. She could've killed her daughters, too.

Escaping Nicole

Franco escaped by taking a few things with him when he went to work, making sure that she didn't notice. He left work early, bought a bus ticket and went to stay with a cousin who lived out of state. The next day, Franco's cousin found him a place to stay until Nicole stopped looking for him. He was so terrified of what she would do that he disconnected his phone and didn't leave the house for a week. He reached out to one of his friends at work a couple weeks later. He found out that she had been searching for him in a rage and threatening his coworkers with deportation for not telling her where he was. Franco hid for months, afraid that she would find out where he was and try to ruin his life.

Franco's Problem

After Franco left Nicole, the best thing for him would have been to apply for VAWA immediately so he could begin the process to get his work permit and social security number and also to obtain his driver's license. Given Nicole's aggressive nature, Franco worried that Nicole would find him and either hurt him physically or have him deported. Now that Franco was no longer in the abusive relationship, he needed to take action to get his permanent residency so he wouldn't have to worry about being deported.

However, like most domestic violence victims, Franco was in a situation where he was just trying to survive. He didn't think about going to an attorney to help him get United States permanent residency. He just wanted to be as far away from Nicole as possible.

Why Mistreated Men Struggle to Ask for Help

Although seeking help is hard enough for any victim of domestic violence, men especially have a hard time because they don't know if anyone will believe them. They worry that no one will believe them when they say that their female partner or spouse abuses them. This is because society, and particularly the Hispanic culture, frowns upon a man that cannot stand up for himself. It is expected that the man is the authoritative figure in the marriage.

Many times, men will have trouble expressing how they were abused by their female spouse. People have the idea that a man will not have to worry about physical or sexual abuse by a woman. Also, isolation, manipulation, and economic control are difficult to explain when society expects the man to have control over themselves and their household.

In Franco's case, there was a lot that Franco could have done to protect himself from Nicole before and after they were together. Franco could have called the police as he did not have to worry about being deported simply because he was undocumented. It would have been best for Franco either to request a Spanish-speaking police officer or to have someone there that would interpret for him in English. This would have allowed Franco to tell his side of the story instead of being overshadowed by Nicole.

If Franco did not want to call the police on Nicole, he could have either looked for help at a battered spouse shelter or filed a restraining order against Nicole. Either of these options would have protected Franco from enduring any more abuse. There are battered spouse shelters that accept men, and they provide the same help and assistance as they do for women in the same situation. Also, a restraining order would have kept Nicole legally away from him. When filing for a restraining order, Franco could have stated why he was filing. He could have stated that it was because of her abuse and described the things she had done.

Franco could also have sought help from the children's school regarding the abuse that the children witnessed and fell victim to. Schools help not only the children but also the family member that is suffering from abuse. Franco did not even have to report the abuse to the school himself; he could have encouraged Nicole's daughters to do it on their own.

How We Helped Franco

Franco had been separated from Nicole for several years before hearing about VAWA. Not only was he hiding from Nicole, he was also hiding from immigration. He thought his chances of obtaining permanent residency had died along with his and Nicole's marriage.

We did not refer to Franco as a victim. VAWA Self-Petitioners don't normally tend to see themselves as a victim because they see someone who is a victim as helpless. They see themselves as a person who suffered from abuse, and they don't want the abuse to define them.

Franco's process to obtain the VAWA Visa was quite simple in terms of the steps he had to take. The VAWA Self-Petitioner must provide certain documents and must give their written testimony regarding the abuse. The attorney does the rest.

We helped Franco with his biggest struggle, which was acknowledging that he was a victim of domestic violence and talking about it. Since Franco is a man, he didn't see himself as a victim. Even though he did not think that Nicole's actions were appropriate, he still considered her behavior part of normal marital problems. This caused an issue because when he was first asked if he was a victim of abuse by his wife, he answered that he was not. However, Franco did say that they had marital problems.

We have found that in most situations where the victim openly and willingly discusses the abuse, it is because they are aware of the VAWA process. The victim understands that speaking about the abuse is the only way that an attorney will be able to determine if the abuse was sufficient to qualify the victim for VAWA. The victim also understands that they must speak of the abuse despite how embarrassing or humiliating it might be for them.

We helped Franco get over the struggle of speaking to us about the abuse. He started by simply mentioning that Nicole would yell and get angry. As we asked more questions about her behavior toward him when she was angry, Franco started to slowly open up about how aggressive she was toward him. We had to get very specific in our questioning and ask if she had done specific things to him. He felt more comfortable answering yes or no to our questions than bringing up the abuse and discussing it in detail. It wasn't until after much questioning that we also found out that Nicole was on drugs and that she had driven them into a ditch, putting their lives—including her children's—in danger.

We made Franco feel comfortable about telling his story by referring to the abuse as "marital problems." We do this for other males that come to us with a similar situation. For example, we will not ask whether there was *abuse* in the relationship because we will typically get a quick "No!" Instead, we ask if there were *marital problems* in the relationship. This will usually lead to a quick "Yes." *Problems* just seem much easier to discuss than abuse.

Once the victim has admitted that there were problems in the marriage, we ask the victim to give us a general idea of what type of marital problems there were. At first, most victims will mention things such as yelling, cursing, and temper tantrums. Then, we start to ask the more specific questions about the abuse. We'll ask the victim if they were ever punched, slapped, kicked, bitten, dragged, etc. We have a list of abuse questions that we go through with each victim. This allows the victim to quickly and easily answer yes or no rather than having to discuss the events.

With Franco, we asked him specific questions that helped him tell his story. Asking specific questions about the abuse also helps victims to *remember*, because some have been through so much abuse for such a long period of time that they have forgotten the details of what they endured.

VAWA Has Nothing to Do with Any Case the Spouse May Have Started

Franco knew that his immigration process had been initiated, but Nicole had never allowed the process to proceed. There was never a decision made about whether Franco, being the spouse of a United States citizen, was approved for permanent residency. The process that Nicole initiated was a family petition, which is the process by which a United States citizen or permanent resident helps a family member obtain United States permanent residency.

When Franco came to our office seeking assistance to gain permanent residency, he found it very difficult to understand VAWA. He assumed that VAWA was a way to continue the immigration process he had started with Nicole. When we explained that it was a *separate* process that had nothing to do with the family petition that Nicole had initiated, he still expressed concerns about what needed to be done about the family petition left lingering.

Like Franco, many clients find it difficult to understand that VAWA is a Humanitarian Visa that has nothing to do with a family petition. The two processes are completely different. The two processes are filed with different immigration departments, they have different requirements, and they do not intersect in any way as they are being processed.

What's more, once a family petition is approved, it will be closed by immigration after a year if the next step in the process is not filed. Usually, the approval of the family petition alone does not grant the beneficiary any benefits other than permission to proceed to the next step in the process. The next step in the process will be different depending on the beneficiary's life history. If the next step is not filed, then the family petition is automatically closed.

In Franco's case, the family petition was approved years earlier and had long been closed by immigration for lack of anyone filing the next step in the process. However, Franco still had several concerns. He wanted to know whether he needed to contact immigration about the old family petition to withdraw the case. He feared that having two cases filed at the same time with immigration would ruin his chances of having the latter case approved. Franco also wondered if his chances of having his VAWA case approved would increase or decrease because of the family petition's approval years earlier.

Franco's concerns are quite common but there is little to worry about. Again, a family petition closes automatically a year after it has been approved and the next step is not filed. There is nothing anyone must do if the beneficiary decides to proceed with a different immigration process. This is so even if the beneficiary decides to proceed with a family petition initiated by a different United States citizen or permanent resident petitioner.

You Can Have More than One Case Pending

Contrary to what many believe, having more than one case filed with immigration will not hurt the applicant's chances of approval. Instead, each case will help the applicant have one more chance of being approved. Once one of the cases that allows the applicant to obtain permanent residency is approved, then the others are withdrawn if they are still pending. However, if the case that is approved first will *not* lead to permanent residency, then the applicant will want to leave the other pending cases alone. This gives the applicant an opportunity to have a work permit while still pursuing permanent residency with one of the pending cases.

As for a family petition that was approved in the past, it does not help or hurt the VAWA Self-Petitioner's chances of having their VAWA case approved. Many clients express this concern because they assume that if they are no longer with the United States citizen or permanent resident spouse, their chances of having any case approved will decrease. This assumption comes from the misunderstanding that the VAWA and family petition requirements are the same, in that they both require the United States citizen or permanent resident spouse to help the undocumented spouse with the process—but that is not the case. On the other hand, other clients assume that if their family petition was approved, their chances of being approved for a different process will increase. However, this assumption is also false.

Was Franco Better off Not Filing for VAWA?

Filing for a visa does not increase your chances of being deported. It is living undocumented in the United States that increases your daily chances of being deported. Therefore, whether Franco was living with Nicole or not, as long as he remained undocumented, he was at risk of being deported. However, the fact that Nicole was vindictive and threatened to call immigration on him to have him deported could have resulted in him facing deportation proceedings.

Every Question Is Important to Ask

Fortunately, Franco asked the questions and didn't let the doubts and fears keep him from moving forward with his case like so many victims do. Many victims won't ask the questions they have regarding their fears because they are embarrassed to ask or they are afraid that if they ask, they will be told exactly what they don't want to hear. These victims will allow their fear of the unknown to overwhelm their desire to pursue an opportunity to gain legal status.

Many of these preconceived ideas of how their immigration case is supposed to play out or how their case may be affected are a result of rumors.

The rumors are started by people who get their information from the news or they google information. Others will go on preaching the rumors as if they were truth because they once went and saw an immigration attorney for a consultation regarding their situation. Then, that person tries to play attorney to anyone that wants to begin an immigration process and is willing to listen.

What's more disturbing is how far from the truth the rumors really are. Usually, they completely miss the mark. With the rumors, it is common for the requirements of the different case processes to be intermingled or confused, thus resulting in false information.

VAWA Self Petitioners Don't Need Anyone to Petition for Them

Another common misunderstanding with VAWA is that the VAWA Self-Petitioner must apply with the assistance of their abusive United States citizen or legal resident spouse. The victim is afraid that the spouse will either refuse to begin, refuse to continue, or stop their VAWA case entirely. However, the abusive spouse does *not* have to find out that the victim is applying and has *no* control over the case even if they do find out.

The Abuser Does Not Control the VAWA Case

In this case, Franco was afraid that Nicole would find out that he was applying for VAWA. He figured that if she knew about it, she would do everything in her control to put a stop to it in order to keep him from being able to obtain legal status. This was such an overwhelming fear for Franco because he knew how aggressive Nicole was. If he had not asked the question regarding his concern, this would have been the reason for him not moving forward and applying for VAWA.

Don't Make Up Requirements that Don't Exist in the Law

Sometimes people *make up* requirements for a case. Humanitarian Visa requirements are most commonly confused with the family petition requirements. Family petitions require one to have a financial sponsor and in most cases an interview abroad. Therefore, people may automatically assume the same is true for Humanitarian Visas. Even when we explain to people that these are *not* requirements for the Humanitarian Visa, they find it hard to believe. They struggle to understand that Humanitarian Visas are not family petitions.

Other times people make up laws based on individual requirements of certain processes. One common law that is completely made up is the "10-year law." Rumor has it that one can somehow automatically be able to apply for permanent residency simply by having lived undocumented in the United States for at least 10 years. However, the "10-year law" comes from a single requirement that is part of a process called cancellation of removal. This process is only available to people who are in removal proceedings. Then, the 10-year presence in the United States is a requirement along with several other requirements.

To an immigration attorney who is well versed in immigration law, these rumors are absurd, but to a person who is not, these rumors are confused with the law. Unfortunately, rumors and misunderstanding of the law often keep people from taking the first step. Many people never take the first step of consulting with an immigration attorney to find out if they *have* an opportunity to gain legal status because they believe false rumors and then *self-diagnose* their own situation. Inappropriately, they conclude that there is no point in seeking out an attorney because they do not have any options, and then they may pass this false information on to others.

Chapter 6

Camilo's Story

MANY MEN QUALIFY FOR VAWA BASED ON THE
MISTREATMENT THEY HAVE ENDURED FROM THEIR
UNITED STATES CITIZEN OR PERMANENT RESIDENT WIFE

Camilo is married to an abusive United States citizen, Joanna. They are separated because of her drug addiction and her abuse toward Camilo.

How They Met

Camilo and Joanna met through Camilo's cousin who was dating Joanna's friend. They were all at a mutual friend's birthday house party one night when they were introduced to each other. Camilo went over and talked to Joanna, and they immediately hit it off. They talked the rest of the night and exchanged phone numbers.

After that night, they were inseparable. For the next several months, the two spent their time going to dinner and movies and hanging out with friends. Then, they talked about marriage. After several conversations about it, they decided they would get married and move in together.

Camilo got them a one-bedroom apartment where they lived together for the next four years of their marriage.

For the first few months of the marriage, everything was wonderful. Their relationship continued as it had while they were dating. After Camilo got off work, he would come home and take Joanna out to dinner or to visit friends.

However, things began to change and Camilo found out that Joanna was using drugs. Since she didn't work, she would spend most of her day alone at home, and when Camilo came home from work, he would notice that her eyes were glazed and bloodshot. She didn't want to go out, and by the looks of the mess around the house, she hadn't done anything at home all day.

Camilo confronted Joanna one day and asked her if she was using drugs. She told him that she did smoke marijuana and that she had always hidden it from him because she was embarrassed about what he might think of her. They talked about it and agreed that Joanna would stop using drugs since it was affecting their marriage.

Camilo thought that their talk would change things and change their marriage for the better. Everything seemed to go well for a few weeks but then things took a turn for the worse.

One day, Camilo clocked out of work right before lunch because he wasn't feeling well. He walked into the house and went straight to the bedroom so he could lie down. What he walked into was both shocking and heartbreaking. Joanna and the man she had once introduced as her cousin, Matthew, were in bed together naked.

Camilo walked back into the living room and sat on the couch, still shocked by what he had seen. He noticed that the coffee table in front of him had small white lines of cocaine on the glass. A couple of the lines had been snorted, leaving behind scattered dust, but there were still several lines left untouched.

Camilo stood up to leave. Tears welled up in his eyes and he felt his heart breaking. He didn't know what he would do, but he knew that things would never go back to the way they had been. As he walked to the front door to leave, Joanna came running out of the bedroom fully clothed. She grabbed his arm and told him not to leave. Camilo turned to her with tears in his eyes and told her he couldn't stay. He told her it was over between them. Joanna became furious and pulled him hard back into the house. She threatened that she would call immigration if he tried to leave.

Camilo was stunned by her threat. He had told Joanna that being deported was his worst fear because of the traumatizing experience he had when he was crossing the border into the United States. He was just 16 years old at the time and he had been sexually abused by his male guide while crossing into the United States. It was something he had confided in her, and he had never told anyone else.

In that moment, he realized that he didn't know Joanna at all. As Joanna started to speak, he assumed she would beg him for forgiveness, kick her boyfriend out, and they would try to work things out. However, what she said next made him realize that would never happen. He felt like his heart had been ripped out of his chest.

Joanna said that Matthew would be living with them from now on. She said that Camilo would sleep on the couch and Matthew would sleep with her in the bedroom. She threatened to call the police on Camilo if he left the house and they would call immigration and have him deported. Camilo stayed because he felt he had no other option.

Neither Joanna nor Matthew worked. They would spend all day together like honeymooners at home while Camilo worked. Joanna still had access to his bank account and she continued to empty it out for drugs.

Every day was torture for Camilo. It wasn't long before the word got out about Camilo's home life situation. His coworkers would make fun of him about financially supporting and living with his wife and her lover. Then, Camilo would come home from work and listen to Joanna complain and curse at him over the simplest things. Camilo couldn't say anything to her; otherwise she would immediately threaten him with calling the police. She would remind him that he was undocumented and no one would believe him over her. She would say that she was going to hurt herself and then call the cops and blame it on him. Camilo was terrified of her.

The Escape

Camilo finally had enough when Joanna tried to have sex with him. Camilo refused her and pushed her away. Camilo asked her why she was doing this if she was with Matthew. Joanna told him that she wanted to get pregnant because Matthew wouldn't be able to give her a baby. Camilo was disgusted by her.

Camilo couldn't continue living under her control. He had to leave before he did something he would regret. He decided one night to gather a few of his things, and he took them with him the next morning. Instead of going to work, he bought a one-way ticket to go and visit a friend who lived out of state. Joanna wouldn't know to look for him there because he had never told her about that friend, who had been with him when he crossed the border.

Camilo's Problem

Camilo was terrified of the threats that Joanna made about calling immigration on him. Being deported was his worst fear and Joanna knew that because he had confided in her. She knew exactly how to manipulate him and control him. She needed him around to financially support her and her lover. She also needed him to get her pregnant so she could start her own family. Camilo was Joanna's puppet and all her intentions were self-centered.

How We Helped Camilo

Camilo contacted us, desperately seeking a way to obtain legal status. He still lived in fear of Joanna, even though it had been several years since he had escaped. He feared that if she found out where he was, she would do everything in her power to have him deported. He knew she would have no sympathy for him. According to Camilo's friends and family, after Camilo escaped, Joanna went around accusing him of having abandoned her and not fulfilling his duty as a husband to financially provide for his wife. Obviously, Joanna felt no remorse for her actions.

We explained to Camilo that VAWA was an option for which he qualified. Camilo's eyes filled with tears of joy because for years he had hoped for an opportunity to gain legal status. He saw obtaining legal status as the opportunity to remove the invisible chains that Joanna still had attached to him. It would free him from her control and he would no longer have to fear her threats.

Chapter 7

Mauricio's Story

Adan is a United States citizen. He is now 25 years old, but he still lives at home with his father Mauricio. Adan has lived with his father most of his life as his mother left the family home when he was 15 years old. As a single parent, Mauricio has raised Adan and given him as much love and attention as he could.

Adan's childhood was what you would consider a normal childhood. He loved school and did well. Adan's mother was also living in the home until Adan went to high school. Both Mauricio and Adan's mother attended all of Adan's school functions and sport events. There weren't any concerning issues with Adan aside from the normal preteen and teen phases.

However, soon after Adan's mother abandoned the home, Adan started to act out at school. Adan stopped doing well academically and he quit all his sports. After school, while Mauricio was still at work, Adan would not come home; instead, he would hang out with his friends until nighttime. When Mauricio questioned him about his whereabouts, he ignored Mauricio.

At home, Adan disobeyed Mauricio constantly, and he became defiant when Mauricio tried to discipline him. Adan didn't contribute in any way to helping Mauricio with chores around the house, and he was spending less and less time at home as the months went by.

Things took a turn for the worse one day when Mauricio searched through Adan's bedroom and found some drugs hidden in his dresser. When Mauricio tried to talk to Adan about what he was doing, Adan pushed his father and told him to mind his own business. Adan's actions shocked Mauricio and broke his heart. He decided to avoid what could turn into a physical altercation and he left the house. Later that evening, he returned home and Adan was gone.

A few days later, Mauricio confronted Adan about his drug use. Without warning, Adan slapped Mauricio multiple times. Immediately, Mauricio called the police and Adan was arrested for domestic violence. That incident was the first of many more to come that would result in Adan punching, kicking, and biting Mauricio. The last and worst incident was when Adan body slammed Mauricio on the driveway and started kicking him. A neighbor saw what was going on and called the police.

A Plan for Escape

After the incident, Mauricio decided to do something about his legal status because he would need to move out of his home to get away from Adan. Since Mauricio was undocumented, until he could gain legal status, it would be difficult to move and create the life he wanted to have, away from Adan's abuse.

Mauricio's Problem

Mauricio has been suffering from Adan's abuse for a decade now, ever since Adan was 15 years old. Adan was arrested for abusing his father, but now he has been released and Mauricio has allowed Adan to return home.

Mauricio once hoped he could mend their relationship since he is the only parent that Adan has. However, Mauricio has now come to realize that there is no hope for their relationship until Adan decides to change.

How We Helped Mauricio

Mauricio contacted our office after listening to one of our online informational videos about VAWA. He had never heard about VAWA before, and he didn't know that it was an option for undocumented parents that have American children who don't want to help them gain legal status. Mauricio contacted us, hopeful that VAWA would be an option for him. Although Mauricio had never asked Adan for help with gaining legal status, Adan had told Mauricio many times that he would never help him with his immigration process, even after he turned 21 years old. The day that Mauricio contacted our office, Adan was 25 years old and had never petitioned for Mauricio.

Mauricio's main concerns were whether filing for VAWA could harm Adan in any way and whether Adan could find out about his VAWA application. Mauricio, still the caring father, was concerned that his VAWA application could prevent Adan from attending college or getting job opportunities in the future. Mauricio was also concerned about what Adan would do to him if he found out that his father had applied for VAWA.

We assured Mauricio that filing for VAWA would not harm Adan in any way, that it would not affect Adan's chances of getting accepted into a college or gaining employment. Also, the fact that someone is named as an aggressor in a VAWA case is not listed on any of the aggressor's records or background checks. Furthermore, the aggressor is not alerted or contacted in any way regarding being mentioned in the VAWA case as the aggressor.

VAWA Summary

VAWA is for undocumented children, spouses, or parents whose United States citizen or permanent resident parent, spouse, or son/daughter respectively will not help them gain legal status and mistreat the undocumented family member. One must establish that the relationship exists or existed. For divorced self-petitioners applying because of their abusive ex-spouses, the divorce must be less than two years old. Additionally, the applicant must be living with, or must have lived with, the abuser. Finally, the applicant must have suffered some type of abuse by their parent, spouse, or son/daughter.

The applicant can gain legal status inside of the United States without having an interview abroad. There is no need for a petitioner or a sponsor, which is unlike the family petition. The aggressor has no control over the case and isn't notified in any way that the self-petitioner is applying for VAWA. Also, the aggressor is not harmed in any way because the VAWA is filed. Required proof of the abuse is only the applicant's written testimony.

The next step is to apply for permanent residency based on the approved VAWA. Residency is obtained inside of the United States without having an interview abroad. Again, no petitioner or sponsor is required because the residency is based on the approved VAWA.

Chapter 8

Everything You Need to Know About T Visas and Human Trafficking

GAINING LEGAL STATUS BECAUSE YOU'RE FORCED
TO WORK OR TO COMMIT A COMMERCIAL SEX ACT

When you hear the word *human trafficking*, you probably imagine something like what you have seen in a movie. You're probably imagining a person who is locked in a room with no food or water and is only let out to work while chained to prevent escape. This person was likely kidnapped and sold into today's modern-day slave trade—human trafficking. Although those situations do exist, typical accounts of human trafficking are much different but can be just as traumatizing.

Our clients are usually not kidnapped and sold into human trafficking. Their human traffickers are the coyotes who help them cross the border into the United States. Their human trafficker is sometimes their boss at their new job. And sometimes their human trafficker is their very own spouse or family member.

Our clients are not living locked in a room chained to a wall. They are living among us. They shop at the grocery stores where we buy our food. They do their laundry at the laundromats that we use. They show up to work at businesses in our communities. They're part of families that we see together at events or in town. They don't look, speak, or act any different than any other person we pass in public. Many times, we know them or have seen them and we have no idea that they are or were a human trafficking victim.

Also, many of our would-be clients have escaped the trafficking situation years ago and have been able to move on with their lives. However, they have no idea that they can obtain legal permanent residency through a T Visa because of what they have suffered. Therefore, they may be living in fear that they will be caught and sent back to their country.

What does it mean to be forced to work or to perform a commercial sex act?

Let's begin by addressing what does not qualify as being "forced to work." It is not forced labor when a person is forced to cook their own food, clean up after themselves, or work for wages to financially support themselves or their family. However, it is forced labor when a person must do those things against their will for someone else. The victim is forced to do the work against their will because they have been harmed physically to get them to work, they have been threatened with harm to themselves or others if they don't work, or they are forced to work using intimidation or verbal abuse.

As for being forced to perform a commercial sex act, the sex act must be performed in exchange for something of value. It does not have to be in exchange for money. It can be in exchange for food, a place to live, clothing, or anything else that is of value.

People sometimes fail to see themselves as victims even though they are performing labor or commercial sex acts against their will because they feel it is their responsibility.

Labor trafficking victims sometimes do not see themselves as victims because they believe they are responsible for fulfilling a debt owed to the trafficker. Even though the labor may not have been a part of the original agreement, the victim will feel a sense of duty to do all that the trafficker demands. This may be the case even when the victim has paid the trafficker financially.

Sex trafficking victims that are forced by their spouses or boyfriends to perform commercial sex acts either with them or with other people may also feel a sense of responsibility to their partner. Depending on their culture, they may feel it is their obligation as the female in the relationship to do as their male partner demands. Even though the victims perform the sex acts against their will, their sense of duty keeps them from identifying as victims.

Force, fraud, or coercion must have been used to induce the person to perform the commercial sex act or perform the work.

What does it mean to be induced by force, fraud, or coercion?

Examples of force include threats to use weapons to cause harm or causing harm with the use of weapons. Physical beatings and threats of physically beating or abusing someone can also be used as force. Raping or threatening to rape a person is considered force. Additionally, physically restraining a person to prevent their escape is considered force.

Fraud occurs when the victim is deceived by the trafficker who takes unjust advantage of the victim. The trafficker may promise an escape from an abusive or poverty-stricken home. In many situations, "coyotes" will guarantee a safe arrival to the United States. Some traffickers will promise future legal immigration status. In some situations, the trafficker will establish a romantic relationship with the victim and then use the relationship to take advantage of the victim. Other traffickers will lie about jobs or opportunities that do not exist. Others post false advertisements about the work that will be required. Some traffickers that are business owners may misrepresent salaries and working conditions. Others may pay significantly less or not pay at all for work performed. In many cases, temporary H2A/H2B workers are lied to about the living conditions, necessities provided, and earning potential.

Coercion is when a person is persuaded to act involuntarily based on threats or intimidation that instill fear of the consequences if they do not act. Initially, the trafficker may exploit a romantic or a familial relationship to lure the victim. Then, the trafficker may threaten the victim, the victim's children, or other family members with harm if the victim does not act. The trafficker may take the victim's identification card, birth certificate, or passport to prevent the victim from escaping. Additionally, the trafficker may isolate the victim and prevent any contact with family members or others and will usually keep the victim under constant surveillance. If the victim is a minor, the trafficker will likely deny the victim's access to education. Restricting the victim's access to food and necessities to create a dependency on the trafficker is common. Threatening the victim with deportation or the police is also common. Typically, the victim is denied any access to medical care. In most cases, the victim is mistreated verbally, emotionally, and psychologically.

In a workplace, the trafficker may demand unreasonably high quotas from the victim. The trafficker may have the victim working in dangerous conditions without the appropriate safety gear or equipment. The victim will likely work long hours every day of the week.

If the victim hired the trafficker as a coyote, the trafficker may force a huge debt upon the victim to prevent the victim from escaping. The trafficker may also exploit the victim's limited English skills to take advantage of the victim. The trafficker may also use his association with a gang to intimidate the victim. Other victims held captive with the victim may be either harmed or abandoned in a remote area if they try to escape, thus serving as an example.

In a relationship, the trafficker may exclude the victim from the immigration process and prevent the victim from obtaining legal status. For victims that have a visa, the trafficker may prevent the victim from renewing an expired visa. The trafficker may also cause the victim to feel shame about their undocumented immigration status.

There must be an element of fear of harm.

The victim must not have been able to leave the situation for fear that the trafficker would cause them physical harm or fulfill their threats. The victim must have remained in the situation either because they were physically forced to stay or because the victim feared the trafficker would hurt them.

Threats of losing one's job if they do not work or if they do not work faster is not by itself sufficient. Companies and employers have the right to require an employee to work or they can otherwise fire the employee. An employee may be told to work faster if they are required to meet a quota. Quotas are also not sufficient for a T Visa.

What if I was being paid to do the work?

Many human trafficking victims are paid to work. The fact that someone is paid to do the work does not weaken the case. Whether someone was paid to do the work does not affect the case.

What if I was never held captive?

Being *physically* held against your will is not a requirement. In other words, no one must hold the victim captive using ropes and chains. The idea that a victim of human trafficking must be held in a locked up windowless room with no way to escape is a scene for the movies. That is not how it generally works in real life. However, a person must be doing the work against their will. Again, this could be the result of a threat to cause the victim harm or cause harm to someone close to the victim.

What if I have already escaped the trafficking situation?

It is required that the person has not left the United States since escaping the trafficking situation.

This one can be confusing to people who have entered the country multiple times undocumented. People assume that multiple undocumented entries will keep them from meeting this requirement. However, multiple entries prior to the trafficking incident are forgiven. However, it is important to remain within the United States after *escaping* the recent trafficking incident. Do not exit the United States. Instead, you should immediately apply for a T Visa.

WHAT HAPPENS AFTER I APPLY FOR THE T VISA?

✓ 30 DAYS AFTER SUBMITTING YOUR APPLICATION TO IMMIGRATION, **YOU WILL RECEIVE A RECEIPT INDICATING THAT YOUR CASE IS PENDING.**

✓ 60 DAYS AFTER SUBMITTING YOUR APPLICATION TO IMMIGRATION, **YOU WILL RECEIVE YOUR BIOMETRICS APPOINTMENT.**

✓ YOUR CASE WILL BE PROCESSED ACCORDING TO THE PROCESSING TIMES LISTED ON THE USCIS.GOV WEBSITE, **THEN YOU WILL RECEIVE A DECISION ON YOUR CASE.**

Processing times are approximate.

HONEST IMMIGRATION.

Chapter 9

Renata's Story

Renata came from Mexico. She had to get out of that country at all costs to help her family that was literally starving. With no work available in the remote area where they lived, there wasn't any money available to buy food. There also wasn't any money to move to another town to find work. Her parents were older and their health was deteriorating for lack of nourishment. They couldn't financially support themselves, much less support Renata. Renata was their only hope for the chance of survival.

In 2005, after having tried her best to find work in her country, Renata looked for options to find work in the United States. She heard that United States H2A work visas were being issued for people to work on farms. This visa was a real option to go work in the United States. Renata would not have to cross the border illegally. She could do things the right way.

Luckily, she was chosen to work in the United States, and she did not have to find a coyote to smuggle her across the border. It was done legally, and she arrived by bus to South Carolina. Once she arrived, the job scout that recruited all the workers took them to their living quarters.

Around midnight, she and 11 other people were driven to a trailer park where their unfurnished single wide mobile home waited. After the long and tumultuous journey, they all went to sleep on the floor since there were no beds.

The next morning they were expected to be up and ready to work at 5:00 a.m. Mando, the man who hired them, arrived in a large school bus transformed into a work bus. He introduced himself quickly and said he hoped they had packed their lunch because it was going to be a long day. Everyone was shocked because they had just arrived hours earlier and didn't have a chance to buy groceries.

Fear of Trafficker

About a month after they began work, Renata was assigned to work on top of the field truck handing out tickets to workers who dumped their produce-filled buckets into the bins on the truck. She stood in the bins on the truck all day and was expected to hand out tickets even while the truck moved between the crop rows. She also had to be quick and move between the bins as they were filled with produce. There wasn't a safety harness or anything to stay balanced.

Renata found it difficult to balance because the truck jerked forward constantly. She had to use both hands to hold and hand out the tickets. So she wasn't able to hold on to the side of the bin. During one of her jumps between a full bin to an empty bin, she lost her balance and fell several feet off the truck.

She landed on her back and felt the pain shoot through her body. The pain was so intense she couldn't get up.

Mando saw what happened and just ignored her. He told the workers that gathered around her to get back to work.

Renata knew then how dangerous it was for her to work there. After some time, she managed to get herself up. She knew she needed to see a doctor. She waited in the work bus until the end of the day when Mando drove all of the workers home.

The next day, after a night of sleeping on the floor, Renata was so sore she could barely move. She had one of her co-workers tell Mando that she would not be able to work that day because she was in so much pain.

Mando got off the bus and went inside to find Renata. He told her that he had not paid to get her to the United States so that she could relax and be on vacation. He threated to call immigration on her if she was not on the bus the next morning ready for work. She started crying and told him she needed to see a doctor because her arm was swollen and her body ached tremendously. He laughed at her and told her that she wasn't going to make it working in the United States if she made a big deal over a little fall.

Years later, she continues to have back pain. She never saw a doctor about her fall.

Exploited

Working conditions were dangerous. The pay was only $100 per week and Mando yelled and insulted the workers all day long. Renata worked from 5:00 a.m. until sunset every day. She would get home exhausted, in pain, with only the floor to lay on.

While working in the tobacco fields, Renata got a rash all over her body. She had migraines and vomited for three days. Again, Renana told Mando she needed to see a doctor. He looked at her and told her she needed to either get back to work or she'd go back to where she came from.

Time to Escape

After Mando denied her medical attention a second time, she knew she had to escape him. This couldn't end well for her. On the other hand, she knew she needed to work to keep her family fed in Mexico.

There was another female coworker who was also tired of Mando's abuse. Renata befriended her and one day while discussing how terrible their situation was, they came up with a plan so that she could escape.

On the day they had planned for their escape, Renata grabbed what little she owned and put it in a plastic bag. The next afternoon while being dropped off at home from work at sunset, together they left the home without telling anyone else where they were going. They walked through the night and never turned back.

Renata's Problem

Renata had come to the United States legally to work. Once in the United States, she followed directions and fulfilled her end of the deal. She knew that she wasn't being treated right, but she didn't know if it was allowed for her to be treated this way since she had nothing to compare this treatment to.

Like most people who come to the United States on temporary work visas, Renata didn't know if she had any rights because she was not a United States citizen. And she believed that she needed her employer's permission to get the medical attention she needed.

Many people that come to the United States on a temporary foreign worker program end up being victims of human trafficking. One of the issues is that no one checks in on the foreign workers once they arrive to make sure they are being treated properly, as is required by law.

These foreign workers are unaware of how they should be treated. They have no one to ask for help. They are isolated from society and their daily routines are controlled by the United States employer. And many times, their identification documents and passports are taken by their employer so as to hold them captive.

How We Helped Renata

Renata heard about the T Visa from a friend that knew the trafficking situation she had been in. Luckily, the friend had learned about the T Visa from our informational videos on Facebook, and she encouraged Renata to seek us out. Renata followed us on Facebook, learning more about the T Visa before contacting our office.

Renata contacted us and explained to us her human trafficking situation and how she had suffered. She wanted to know if there was any way that she would be able to gain legal status based on her situation. Although it had been years since she had escaped Mando, she still suffered physically because Mando had not gotten her the medical attention she needed immediately after her injury.

We made Renata aware that she qualified for the T Visa. Renata's biggest concern was fear that Mando would harm her or her family because she was filing a T Visa. We explained to her how the T Visa works and that she had nothing to fear because Mando would likely not find out about it. Renata was hugely relieved and she applied for the T Visa.

Chapter 10

Hugo's Story

A T VISA OFFERS A FRESH START
FOLLOWING HELLISH WORK CONDITIONS

A company from the United States came to Hugo's hometown in Mexico where they recruited men to work under foreign worker visas.

He was told that they were looking for men to work on farms and showed them brochures of men working happily. Everything looked great.

They were told that the work would be seasonal but if they were good workers, they would renew their visas every year.

They promised room and board, daily meals, and everything they needed for work upon arrival.

The workers would have to pay for their travel expenses to the United States and sign a contract so the employer could hire them.

Hugo thought this opportunity was a blessing. He borrowed money from a family member and gave him the title to his parent's property as collateral. He knew he'd be able to pay him back shortly after beginning work in America.

Upon arrival in the United States, Hugo knew immediately that something wasn't right. He was placed in a two-bedroom apartment with nineteen other men. There were a few bare, twin-sized mattresses scattered throughout the apartment, but not enough for everyone. Some men slept two to a mattress to avoid sleeping on the floor. He had to sleep on the floor using his clothing as a pillow and blanket. It was difficult to walk in the apartment with the mattresses on the floor and people's belongings.

There was no way to call his family since no one had a cell phone. In a way, he was glad he couldn't speak to his parents because he wouldn't be able to hide how scared he was.

They were all picked up for work early the next morning but only a bucket was provided once they got to the farm. No breakfast, no gloves, no opportunity to call home. They started work on an empty stomach.

It was their first time in the United States and they were scared. None of them spoke English. They didn't know where to find help.

Hugo and the men soon learned that the company lied about everything. Days went by and they still hadn't been taken to buy groceries or do their laundry. But even if they had bought groceries, the twenty workers had one stove to cook on and one fridge to store everyone's food.

The men worked picking tomatoes. It was summer, and the sun was scorching hot. Their skin was burning because they didn't have hats or handkerchiefs to cover themselves. They got home sunburned and blistered. They didn't have time to heal before it was back to work the next day.

Their promised daily meals consisted of two bean and egg tacos, two for breakfast and two for lunch. The men had to fend for themselves for dinner. Since cooking meant waiting two to three hours before getting a turn to use the stove, Hugo usually ate a cold can of soup with some bread for dinner.

Using the restroom was another challenge. Showering before bed or getting ready in the morning could take a couple of hours because there was only one bathroom. Every morning, Hugo woke up a couple hours early just to make sure he was ready for work on time.

At work, they were constantly being threatened with immigration if they didn't work fast enough. They also threatened not to pay them if they didn't complete their rows. They had one 30 minute break for lunch and that was it. Those who took frequent water breaks were ridiculed for not being man enough to stand the heat.

Threats weren't the only abuse they suffered. The supervisors would throw tomatoes at the workers if they thought the men were working too slow. They'd curse at men who stopped to take a quick break and insulted them in front of everyone.

Hugo worked in pain because his body was burned and blistered, especially his hands because he hadn't been given any gloves to carry the heavy buckets.

The men were all told they would not see a paycheck until they made it through the 30-day probation period.

Hugo felt weak from hunger and sleep deprivation. His body was always in pain. He had constant headaches from the heat. He felt some relief at times when his blistered hands would go numb. He still hadn't spoken to his family since he arrived. He worked from sunrise to sunset every day. The company treated them like animals and they had no where to turn to for help.

The Escape

One of the men in the group asked Hugo if he wanted to escape with him. The man was planning his escape and wanted others to go with him. He told Hugo he couldn't stay because he would probably end up dead from exhaustion. Hugo knew he was right.

One morning at 2:00 a.m., they both woke up and left. They walked for hours until they reached a shopping center where there were pay phones they could use. Hugo contacted his family members who were in the United States. His family sent him money to get a bus ticket to their home eight hours away.

Hugo's Problem

Hugo was in a similar situation as Renata. He did everything right and didn't break any laws to get into the United States. But after he arrived, he discovered that he had been lied to about everything, including pay, living conditions, working conditions, and necessities provided.

What may be even more shocking to people who are unaware of how foreign worker programs work is that the company that brought Hugo to the United States did so with permission from United States Immigration. The United States company lied to United States Immigration about how it would pay, house, and use Hugo and the others for work. However, no one ever followed up with the company to make sure that once these men were in the United States, they were being treated properly.

How We Helped Hugo

Hugo came to us after hearing our online human trafficking information videos. It had been several years since he had escaped his trafficking situation. However, Hugo wanted justice.

Hugo had since married and now had a child on the way. He lived in fear every day because he was living undocumented in the United States. He knew it would be devastating for his wife if he were deported. His wife was also undocumented and they both feared how it would affect her pregnancy if she was detained while pregnant.

We explained to Hugo that one way he could have justice for what was done to him was in the form of a T Visa for himself to be able to live in the United States legally. He could also include his wife as a derivative in his application so that she could also obtain a T Visa. Hugo's wife could obtain a T Visa just because she was his wife. She did not have to be a human trafficking victim or even have known Hugo when he was a victim.

When Hugo discovered the T Visa as an option to gain legal status, he took the opportunity to apply. Hugo is currently waiting on his pending T

Visa to be processed. He added his wife as a derivative to his T Visa because he wants to make sure that she can gain legal status at the same time that he does. Hugo is extremely relieved that he has found a way to gain legal status for both himself and his wife.

Chapter 11

Maya's Story

When Maya was 16 years old, she met John. Every day after work, she walked home around the same time in the afternoon. John started walking the same route through town that she did. He said he worked near her workplace and got off at the same time. He would walk alongside her and tell her how beautiful she was and try to get her to go out on a date with him.

He invited her to go out on a date with him, and he had to ask several times before Maya accepted his invitation.

On their date night, John picked her up to go to dinner. They had a good time and Maya thought things were going great. After dinner, John told Maya that he was going to take her to meet his sisters. John and his two sisters lived together. When they arrived at his house, he introduced her to his sisters. Immediately, they started to compliment her and asked her questions. Then, Maya asked to use the restroom, and when she was done, she realized John was gone.

Maya stayed there through the night because John's sisters insisted she not leave because the area wasn't safe to walk at night. The next morning, Maya didn't know how to return home to face her parents after leaving with a young man and not returning. Also, John's sisters watched her closely.

John returned home the next day around noon. He apologized profusely and told her there was an emergency, and he had to leave right away. Maya cried and told him that she didn't know how to face her parents since she'd left with him and not returned all night. He parents were traditional and wouldn't accept her after being with a man all night. John comforted her and said that he'd make things right by marrying her.

Maya was overwhelmed with emotions since John was the first boyfriend she'd ever had. Maya took him to her family's home, and John asked her father for her hand in marriage. They married about a week later.

John told Maya that she would no longer work because he would provide for her. The days leading to their marriage, John spent a lot of time with her. However, the day after they married things changed.

John would leave early in the morning and come home around midnight. His sisters were always home. When John wasn't around, they were always watching her. They would tell her that John was gone more because he had to work harder for her. They'd keep her busy by having her help them do things around the house. Anytime Maya wanted to go somewhere, they would convince her not to go.

John started coming home less and less. Some nights he didn't make it home at all.

After a couple of weeks, Maya became desperate to leave the house. She realized she hadn't stepped outside of the house alone since she'd come over the first night.

It wasn't until one morning that Maya woke up earlier than usual that she noticed the front door was locked from the inside. You needed a key to unlock the deadbolt. It was only a few minutes that Maya was up before one of the sisters was asking Maya what she was doing. Her voice sounding more threatening than sweet.

Maya started to feel that something was very wrong.

That very night John came home and told her to pack her bags because they were leaving. John seemed hurried. He hadn't come home the last couple of nights so she hadn't spoken to him much.

He dropped her off with his friend and told her he would meet her on the other side. Maya was confused.

Maya was then taken across the border to the United States to a home where she was to wait for John.

Immediately after arriving at the house, John's friend brought her some lingerie to wear. She was told to put it on or John would be upset with her.

Finally, John showed up. Maya asked him what was going on, and his response stabbed her like a knife in her chest.

He told her the truth. He said that he was in the business of recruiting women, marrying them, and making them work in prostitution.

Maya was devastated by the truth.

John told her that he knew who her family was and where they lived so they would suffer the consequences if she disobeyed him.

Maya was taken to a brothel that night and was forced to work in prostitution.

Although John did not directly supervise Maya, her pimps made it known that they would report directly to John if Maya disobeyed them.

The first time that Maya disobeyed, John beat her severely. John made it clear to Maya that he owned her now. Maya fought back, but her disobedience resulted in beatings every time. Maya witnessed other women in the brothels also being beaten when they didn't obey.

John and the pimps broke her spirit and made her believe that she was worthless and that no one cared enough to look for her. Still a child, Maya believed everything they said.

Maya was locked in a room with no way to escape and was only let out to work or to help clean the brothel. She was only allowed to eat and use the restroom once a day.

Maya lived in fear for her safety and the safety of her family.

John threatened that when he was finished with her, he would kill her where no one could find her body.

Maya was finally able to escape when one of the customers decided to help her. He had seen the bruises on her body and knew she was there against her will. He knew that she was young and that she would never make it out alive without help. One night he helped her sneak out. Then, he found her a place to stay with his family members in a nearby town until she could find a job to earn money and live on her own.

Maya's Problem

Maya came to the United States a child, unwillingly and unknowingly. It was not her decision to come to the United States. She was obligated to come at the demand of her husband, and if she had refused, she would have been forced to come. She would not have had an option because from the time that she lived with her "sisters-in-law," she was already being held in a human trafficking situation unbeknownst to her.

How We Helped Maya

When we met Maya, she had been free from John for over a decade. However, emotionally she still had not gotten over what he had done to her. She sobbed as she described all the horrible things she had been forced to go through.

What was worse was that she had not returned to her home country to visit her family since the day she was forced to come to the United States. She missed them so much, but she feared returning since John had already gone to look for her there. Her family told her to stay away from there because he would kill her if he found her. Still, her family had no idea what he had done to her or put her through. She wasn't even sure if she wanted to face her family because she would need to tell them what had happened. She couldn't bear to think of how they would react.

Maya's main concern was whether John would be able to locate her if she filed for a T Visa. We calmed her worry by explaining to her that the T Visa was designed to protect the victim. It allows victims to use safe addresses. A safe address is an alternative address the victim chooses to use other than the victim's residential address. Maya was greatly relieved to know that she didn't have to provide her residential address on her T Visa application so that neither John nor immigration could locate her. Then, Maya felt comfortable applying for the T Visa.

Maya was approved for the T Visa, and she has been able to obtain a better paying job since she received her T Visa. Now she is waiting for her opportunity to apply for permanent residency under the T Visa. Her plans are to visit her family in her home country once she obtains her residency. She dreams of having her children meet their grandparents for the very first time.

Chapter 12

Jessica's Story

A T VISA AIDS A WOMAN WHOSE HUSBAND
FORCED HER INTO PROSTITUTION

Jessica met Raul in her home country. They dated for a year and then got married. After they got married, Raul decided they should move to the United States to live a better life. Jessica hesitated at first, but Raul convinced her of how much better their lives would be there.

On the way to the United States, Raul started acting differently toward Jessica. He seemed angry and distant. She had never seen this side of him. When they arrived to the United States, the couple moved into Raul's cousin's house. Raul's cousin lived with his wife. The morning after they arrived, Raul's cousin gave him the bad news that he wasn't able to secure a job for him with his friend. To help cheer Raul up, Jessica told Raul she would find a job to get them on their feet.

Immediately after Jessica said she would find a job, Raul told Jessica he had found a job for her already. She could go to work with his cousin's wife. Jessica was confused by his quick response. She had no idea when or how he'd found her a job. He certainly hadn't mentioned this to Jessica, but she figured it was because he had been angry at her. He didn't tell her what type of job it was, but she figured her husband knew what was best for her.

Even more surprising was when he said she would begin working that afternoon. They hadn't even settled in yet. Raul was acting strange. He wouldn't make eye contact with her and he hardly spoke to her. However, she figured the only way they were going to be able to get their own place in the United States was by working hard.

By noon, Jessica still hadn't met the cousin's wife. She overheard him tell Raul that she was still sleeping. Jessica had questions for her about her new job. What should she wear? Would she need to go out and buy anything? What time should she be ready?

Finally, around 5:00 p.m., the cousin's wife came out to the kitchen and started preparing dinner. She looked exhausted even though she'd just slept all day. Jessica approached her and started making conversation. The woman didn't say much. She told Jessica she needed to eat because they'd work late.

They didn't leave until it was dark. Jessica thought it was odd to work at night, but she didn't ask any questions. They drove to a house in a rundown neighborhood. Jessica still didn't know what type of work she'd be doing, but she assumed they were there to clean the house.

They went inside, a woman named Diana took Jessica to a bedroom, walked over to the closet, pulled out some lingerie, handed it to Jessica, and told her to put it on. Immediately, Jessica protested in disgust and refused to put on the lingerie. Jessica demanded to speak to Raul. Diana assured Jessica that Raul knew what type of work Jessica would be doing there.

Jessica stood there in disbelief that she had been taken to a brothel to work as a prostitute. She thought surely her husband was lied to about the work she would be doing there. Surely, his cousin had no idea that his wife worked as a prostitute.

Seeing that Jessica was in shock and still didn't believe her, Diana dialed Raul on the phone and handed it to Jessica. Raul answered and Jessica began to tell him what these insane women expected her to do. Jessica expected Raul to be furious and tell her that he would come and get her right away. Jessica would put an end to this nonsense and her husband would come and teach these women a lesson. However, Jessica was even more shocked by the silence she heard on the other end of the line. Raul calmly told her to do as Diana asked. He said everything would be okay and then he hung up.

Jessica felt nauseous. She couldn't process what had just happened. Was that her husband on the phone that had just told her to stay there, to work there, to listen to Diana?

Diana allowed Jessica to sit in the hallway that night. Jessica watched as Diana supervised the women in the bedrooms. Men came and went from the bedrooms, and Diana charged them before they left.

Jessica couldn't wait to leave so she could explain to Raul what exactly the job entailed. She knew that once he knew the truth, he wouldn't make her go back there ever again.

Finally, at sunrise, Jessica was driven back home. Jessica ran into Raul's arms. Sobbing, she told him that the job was prostitution and that she was sure his cousin didn't know what his wife was doing. She begged him to gather their things and leave immediately.

Raul didn't console her. Instead, he pulled her away from him and told her that she had to do the work and listen to Diana; otherwise, he would make her do it. Jessica had never heard him speak to her that way. She protested and he beat her.

Jessica knew then that she had no idea who this man was when she had married him.

From that day forward, Jessica had to completely obey Diana. If Jessica disobeyed Diana in any way, Raul would be waiting to beat her when she got home. He would beat her so often that her body was covered in bruises.

Working at the brothel was horrific. Jessica had to service up to 20 men a day—sometimes without protection and even while on her menstrual cycle. Some men were abusive and aggressive; those were the worst. Jessica and the women working at the brothel were forbidden to speak to anyone. Diana made sure they didn't speak, and she reported any type of disobedience to their husbands or pimps.

About a week after working at the brothel, Jessica started to have suicidal thoughts. She told Raul about it hoping that he would have some compassion for her. Instead, Raul picked up the phone and threatened to tell her parents what type of work she was doing in the United States. Raul looked at Jessica and asked if she was going to be obedient. Heartbroken and numb, Jessica said yes.

Jessica was not allowed to leave the house without Raul. Their outings were rare. During the day, she would help with the house chores—cooking, cleaning, and laundry—and then at night, Jessica was driven to the brothel to work until sunrise. This was life day in and day out. Jessica had to report to Raul each day how many men she had serviced, and Diana delivered Jessica's earnings to Raul every week.

One day, Jessica showed up to the brothel to work, but Diana wasn't there. A tall young man was there to take her place. She noticed he didn't know what he was doing, and it seemed he was going off what little instruction he'd been given.

After servicing one of her customers, she noticed that no one was at the door to charge him. The customer walked out without paying. That had never happened before. Jessica threw some clothes on and looked down the hall. The young man was nowhere in sight. She chased after the customer and asked him for a ride to the store. She acted as if it was normal for her to just leave the brothel as she pleased. The customer had no idea she was there against her will.

Once she got to the store and the customer drove off, she walked for miles until she came to another store. There, she found someone to help her contact family members in the United States.

Jessica's Problem

Jessica fell in love with a terrible man, a man who had lied to her from the very beginning of their relationship. He wanted to get her exactly where he wanted her, to do what he wanted her to do.

It would be easy to judge Jessica because she came willingly with her husband to the United States undocumented. One could argue that she shouldn't have cared if Raul threatened to tell her family and that she could have tried to escape sooner. After all, it seemed she had so many opportunities to escape each time she rode to the brothel with Raul's cousin's wife. Why couldn't she just have her drop her off at the nearest bus station? Why couldn't they both drive to a police station to report their husbands? Why couldn't Jessica just go to the nearest phone, call her family, and warn them of what she was going thru?

Until you have been in the exact situation Jessica was in, you can't judge her because the truth is that you have no idea what you would do or how you would react. Jessica couldn't have escaped on her own; she had too many people watching her, people who were all benefitting from having her as a slave.

How We Helped Jessica

We met Jessica a few years after she had escaped from Raul. She knew that Raul had not contacted her family because she kept in touch with them frequently, but she didn't dare return to her hometown where she knew that Raul would find her if he got word that she had gone back there. As far as Jessica's family knew, no one had ever come looking for her on Raul's behalf after she left him. Jessica lied to her family and told them that she had separated from Raul only because he was physically abusive, but she didn't tell them about the rest of the abuse. She begged them not to let anyone know where she was living in the United States.

Jessica was living in hiding from Raul and in hiding from immigration. She was tired of hiding, and she wanted to find a way to live and work in the United States legally. She didn't see going back to her hometown as an option for years to come because of her fear of Raul.

During our consultation with Jessica, we asked her many questions. When she answered that she had been forced to commit commercial sex acts, we knew we might be able to help her. We asked her more about the situation that involved forcing her to commit the acts. After she told us her story, we knew that she qualified for a T Visa.

Jessica had fears and doubts, but once we explained the T Visa process steps to her, she knew that applying for the T Visa was her best option. She figured that she could either keep hiding from immigration or end up detained by immigration and then deported to her hometown where Raul could then find her. Remaining undocumented seemed like a lose-lose situation that would force her to continue to live in hiding. For her to have a better future free from hiding, she needed to apply.

Chapter 13

Mia's Story

AFTER HELPING WOMEN ACROSS THE BORDER,
COYOTES USE THREATS, TORTURE AND ISOLATION—
AND TAKE AWAY THEIR FREEDOM

Mia met the trafficker, Jaime, through an acquaintance.

Jaime was a coyote, and he told her he could get her across the border. He said he had a higher fee, but he assured her that there wouldn't be any problems crossing safely because he had connections and had done this many times.

On the day of departure, Jaime took Mia to a hotel until he could cross her into the United States. After a few days, he returned to get her and took her to a house with several others. He then told her they would cross that night.

Once in the United States, Mia was dropped off at a house. Mia asked if she could contact her family, but Jaime said that he would contact her family. He told her that she would not be released until the family paid him what he asked. Mia knew then that she was in trouble.

A few days later, Mia was taken to a house where a family lived. She was told that she was there to work for them and do what they said. Then, she was put in one of the bedrooms and locked in. She was told that she would work there until her family paid the money. After Jaime dropped her off, the couple in the home came to her bedroom and told her she would be up early to work and they didn't want any trouble from her. The woman threatened that if she didn't listen, she would be handed over to immigration. She said if Mia tried to escape, they would send the police to hunt her down. Mia felt trapped and helpless.

The woman was cruel. She burned her with spatulas that she would heat on the stove if she felt Mia wasn't working fast enough. There was no way to treat her burns, and she was forced to keep doing house chores despite the unbearable pain. The woman would point the spatula in her face as she ordered her around.

Mia felt like a slave having to wake up every morning before sunrise to cook breakfast and lunch for the man of the house. Then, it was a day filled with cleaning, laundry, and more cooking. She was only given what few leftovers there were after everyone else ate. She couldn't take breaks. She was not allowed to shower because the woman said she wouldn't have her running up her water bill. At night, it was back to being locked in the bedroom. She was exhausted and mistreated, but she had no way to contact her family.

The Escape

One day, after about a couple of months of starvation and torture, a neighbor came by looking for the man of the house. The woman went to look for her husband and left the neighbor waiting outside. Since it was cold, the neighbor decided to wait inside the house and let himself in. The woman had disappeared to the back of the home and still had not returned. Mia was cleaning the living room near the front door and was startled when she saw the neighbor standing there. Mia had been told never to go outside because if someone saw her they would call immigration on her. The man stood there staring at her. He was shocked at the physical condition that Mia was in. He asked who she was as he stared at the burn marks on her arms and legs. Mia didn't reply for fear of getting in trouble.

Mia disappeared into another room out of the man's sight as soon as she heard the man and woman coming. She could hear them chatting. Mia was afraid that the neighbor would tell them that he saw her, but he didn't say a word about Mia. The man walked with the neighbor outside as they continued ther conversation. The woman quickly found Mia and asked if the neighbor had seen her. Mia casually said no to seem believable.

About a week later, the neighbor came over again, but this time with his wife. The woman chatted with them briefly and left them standing outside as she went and fetched her husband. Mia stood silent in a hallway, staying out of sight. Suddenly, the woman appeared in the hallway. If Mia hadn't been so exhausted she would have screamed with fright. The woman scanned Mia's body quickly with her eyes. It's as if she was searching for something. Mia ran to her room afraid of what the woman would do to her if she found out she'd been seen. The woman found the neighbor's wife in the hallway and asked her what she was doing. Mia heard her reply that she was looking for a restroom.

A few days later, a police officer showed up at the house. Mia could hear him threatening the couple that they could either let him look around or he would get a warrant to search the home and it would be much worse for them. The officer found Mia in her bedroom. He asked her who she was and how she'd gotten the burns on her body. Mia didn't answer. Since the couple claimed that she was a friend staying with them until her family could come and get her, the officer offered Mia to help her contact her family. Mia knew that she could either go with the officer and hopefully see her family again or stay with the couple and never see her family again. Mia took the risk of leaving with the officer, who helped her contact her family and never asked about her immigration status.

Mia's Problem

Mia ended up in a situation like many other women that travel alone to the United States with a coyote. Mia's coyote took advantage of the fact that Mia was a female and he saw her as free labor. To him she was someone that he could put to work with the excuse that her family had not paid for them to be released. In these situations, the coyote never contacts the victim's family after arriving in the United States. Other times, the coyote will increase the fee the family owes to keep the victims longer and put them to work. The coyote has full control of the victim by preventing the victim from contacting any family members.

Not only was Mia young and naïve, she was in a foreign country where she didn't know the language or how to find help. For that reason, she was at the mercy of the traffickers to determine when and whether she would see her family again. Having someone constantly supervising her made the possibility of escape much more difficult.

How We Helped Mia

We met Mia when she was a middle-aged woman. She was still living with her parents and caring for them in their old age. She wasn't married and she didn't have any children. Mia hadn't been able to move on with her life after being trafficked. For years, the nightmares and the fear of being found by the traffickers made her live in a panic. Before too long, it became a way of life. Socializing was the most difficult thing for Mia because it meant having to be around people and trusting them with her safety.

Mia came to us desperate to find an opportunity to gain legal status. She hoped it would give her freedom from the psychological harm the traffickers had caused her. She wanted to finally move on with her life and not continue living defined by the trafficking.

Mia's biggest concern was whether we could guarantee 100 percent that she could obtain the T Visa. We explained to Mia that even though we would do our very best work on her case, the approval of the T Visa is out of any attorney's control. There is no way to guarantee an approval. However, there are certain factors that can reduce the applicant's chances of approval. These include: Having a guilty charge including a sexual act or harm to a child on one's criminal record, being affiliated with a gang, being an alcoholic or drug addict, or not qualifying for the relief sought. We explained to her that the fact that she had no criminal record, no affiliation with a gang, she didn't do drugs or alcohol, and she had sought legal advice to determine if she qualified to apply for the T Visa greatly increased her chances of approval.

Chapter 14

Caleb's Story

Caleb met his trafficker, Juan, when he was just 15 years old. He was working in the fields picking produce. Life was tough but he had his freedom. Juan just showed up one day in the field where he was working. He offered the group of people that Juan was working with a chance to make more money working for him in the fields in a different state. He said he would charge them $500 to transport them but they could pay him back once they got there. Many of them went with him the next day.

Caleb knew he had made a terrible decision as soon as he got to his destination because he was crammed into a small one-bathroom mobile home with 14 other people. He had no place to sleep but the floor—no mattress, no pillow, and no blanket so he had to sleep on the bare floor. He was terrified.

There were several men who worked with Juan that lived in the mobile home next to them, and they were there to supervise the newcomers. Immediately, they told Caleb and the others not to try to leave or immigration would be called and they would be deported.

The first morning they went to work, Caleb noticed that things were going to get worse. Juan gave the newcomers instructions for the workday and then started to threaten them with deportation if they didn't obey. Caleb and the others got to work right away. There were no breaks and no water to drink before lunch during the long, hot workday. Lunch was only a quick 20-minute break when they fed the men two slices of bread with a single slice of bologna for the entire work day. Juan and his men drank cold sodas and beer all day long, and the only thing they offered the boys to drink was water from a nearby irrigation hose. That water may not have been for drinking because it had a foul odor, but it was the only option. Caleb drank it anyway because he was so thirsty he felt he would pass out. As the day went on and the workers slowed down because of the scorching heat, the insults got worse. The boys were constantly told that they were worthless, that they were good for nothing, and that the men could do whatever they wanted to them because they were American citizens and the newcomers were not.

One day, Caleb reached a point of paralyzing exhaustion. He was so exhausted he couldn't move. He sat there in the middle of the crop row, put his bucket over his head and passed out. Caleb awoke to Juan pointing a knife in his face yelling at him to get up. Caleb eventually got up and dragged himself around until the end of the day.

Caleb and the others were not paid the money they had been promised. They'd work from sunup to sundown six days a week and only get paid $25 for the week. Juan said he kept the rest because they owed him. Caleb didn't even have enough money to buy food to last him for the week, and he went hungry most days. He washed what few clothes he had together with others to save money on laundry.

On Sundays, they were taken on a bus to a nearby town where they did laundry and bought groceries. But they couldn't even enjoy the day off because Juan and his men were constantly scaring them that immigration was near. Juan would also threaten to report them to immigration himself if they tried to escape. He would always remind them that they had no rights in this country and that he could do whatever he wanted to them.

Caleb believed him because he watched as Juan and his men mistreated the boys daily and no one stopped them. He watched as they beat several of the boys out on the field because the boys were so exhausted from the heat they couldn't lift their buckets anymore. Juan and his men would throw their empty beer bottles at them while they worked if they thought they were not working fast enough.

As badly as they were treated, Caleb was never more terrified of them than the day that he saw what terrible things Juan was capable of. It was on a Sunday. The workers were loading the work bus to head to town to do their laundry and grocery shopping. Caleb had forgotten his wallet and ran back inside to get it. He heard whimpering in the back bedroom. He thought someone might be hurt so he went to see what was going on. The door was cracked and Caleb saw Juan heavily intoxicated fondling one of the other young boys. Caleb felt sick to his stomach. He quickly and quietly walked away afraid to meet the same fate. Caleb loaded the bus feeling hopeless.

Caleb knew he had to get out of there. That same day when they went to the grocery store, he spoke to a couple of men from his home country that he had met there before. The men worked for a farmer at a different farm and would also come to the store on Sundays to do their grocery shopping. One of the men had once asked Caleb if he wanted to come and work for their boss after they found out how little Caleb got paid by Juan. Caleb hadn't even told them how badly they were treated because he was embarrassed. Now Caleb told the man that he wanted to take him up on his offer. Caleb figured it would be a while before they could plan to accommodate him, so he was shocked when the man said Caleb could leave with him that day. Caleb snuck onto the bus with the man and he lay in one of the back seats until the bus was far away from the grocery store. Finally, after five months, his nightmare was over.

Caleb's Problem

Once Caleb was working for Juan, he was stuck there because he feared Juan's daily mistreatment and threats of deportation. He had become a victim of human trafficking and there was no one to stop the abuse. He needed to find a way out.

How We Helped Caleb

We never met Caleb, the kid. We met Caleb, the man. The man who had suffered so much as a trafficked kid that he cried as he retold his story. He felt compassion for the boy in him that had lived that nightmare and he felt anger toward Juan for the harm he'd caused. There we were, more than a decade later, watching as Caleb still hadn't gotten past the hurt and the suffering after being trafficked.

Caleb's biggest concern was whether he would be able to help his wife obtain a T Visa as well. His wife was undocumented and they had three children together. They both lived in fear of deportation and desperately hoped for an opportunity to gain legal status.

We explained to Caleb that he would be able to add his wife as a derivative so long as they were married. It did not matter in what country they had married as long as their marriage was valid. One of the required pieces of evidence for his wife's case would be a copy of their marriage certificate. During the consultation, we found out that Caleb and his wife had never married. They had lived together for seven years and had children together but they had never married. However, this issue was an easy fix. Caleb and his wife had to go to the nearest courthouse to marry in a court of law. The process was simple and fast. Caleb and his wife were married within a couple of weeks, and Caleb added his wife as a derivative for his T Visa.

Chapter 15

Elsa's Story

Javier reached out to Elsa on Facebook. He messaged her and said he was her cousin that also lived in the United States. He lived in a city just a couple of hours away from her. Elsa remembered him from her childhood when they lived in the same home town in Mexico. Elsa confirmed with her older sister in Mexico if this man was indeed their cousin. Elsa also noticed that they had mutual family members as friends on Facebook, so she felt comfortable talking to him.

A few months later, Elsa found herself in financial trouble and she needed to move out of her apartment when both of her roommates decided to move to a different state. Elsa still had frequent communication with Javier, and during a Facebook conversation, she mentioned to him that she needed to move. Quickly, he said that Elsa could move in with him. He said he had a two-bedroom apartment all to himself and he had an extra bedroom. He said that Elsa could come and live rent free until she could get back on her feet.

His offer seemed sincere. He wanted to help her because Elsa was family and she needed help. So she accepted his offer and made plans to move in with him.

The night Elsa arrived at Javier's apartment, he led her to a room that was not a bedroom but more of a laundry room with a mattress on the floor. He looked at her with a smirk and said that the bedroom was all hers. Since she had just arrived, she didn't bother him with all the concerned questions that she had.

The next morning, Elsa realized that there two women were living in the bedroom Javier had said was empty. One woman came out of the bedroom and walked over to her. She looked at Elsa and walked away without saying a word. The woman looked hollow in a disturbing way. Elsa didn't know if they were roommates or just friends who had stayed the night in the spare bedroom.

Both women started making breakfast and cleaning up the apartment in silence. Elsa jumped in the shower, and when she came out, Javier was awake and eating at the table. The women were serving him as if he were a king. He gazed over at Elsa and told her to come over and sit down to eat breakfast. The women didn't make eye contact with her as they served her.

When Javier was done eating, he told her that everyone in that apartment pulled their own weight in paying the bills. He said she would have to do the same. Feeling embarrassed, Elsa told him she'd start looking for work right away to help. She didn't want him to think she expected a handout just because they were family. Javier looked at her with that smirk again. The smirk that made her uneasy and feel as if she should regret being there. He told her that he already had a job for her because he didn't want her out on the street since she was undocumented. He said she would begin work that night. He warned her not to go outside because it wasn't an immigrant friendly city and some of the neighbors were racist. He said if they saw her they would surely report her to immigration to have her deported. According to him, that had already happened several times to neighbors.

After breakfast, Elsa called her parents on her cell phone and told them about her move. Javier saw her on the phone. When she got off the phone, he took it away from her. Elsa thought it was strange but she figured maybe he had run out of minutes on his. When he didn't give it back, Elsa asked him for it. Javier became furious and slapped her across the face. Then, Elsa knew that something was seriously wrong. She wanted to leave but she had no money and nowhere to go.

That afternoon, Javier called the two women and Elsa to the living room. She thought that Javier was going to apologize for his actions earlier. However, Elsa was horrified by what she heard. He instructed the women to get Elsa dressed and ready for work that evening. At first Elsa was confused. Javier noticed that Elsa had no idea what was going on. Javier got in her face and told her that she wasn't a little girl and that he was going to speak to her clearly. He said men would be coming over and pay to have sex with her.

In disbelief, Elsa pushed Javier away from her and walked towards the door. She could take a man slapping her, but she was not going to let men have their way with her. Javier grabbed her by the hair and pulled her to the ground. He dragged her to his bedroom. Elsa fought him until she had no more strength to fight. Then, he raped her. He threatened that if she left he would call her parents and tell them that she had come on to him and had sex with him. Elsa knew that would break her parent's hearts.

Elsa knew she had to find a way out of there as soon as possible. The women got themselves ready for work and they gave Elsa some lingerie to wear. They covered her bruised eye and busted lip with makeup. Javier made Elsa swallow a pill. He told her it would clam her nerves, but she felt light-headed and numb.

The men soon arrived, and Javier took their money at the door. Then, he allowed them to pick a woman and he led them to one of the bedrooms. When a man picked Elsa, Javier led them both to Elsa's room.

She hated her life. She had never thought that her life could lead to this. She had no way to communicate with her family to ask for help, and she felt worthless and alone. This went on for several weeks and Elsa was beaten if she didn't obey Javier. She was forced to commit commercial sex acts and when she wasn't forced to do that, she worked like a slave for Javier doing everything he demanded.

Elsa quickly realized that Javier was the only one who left the apartment. None of the women were allowed outside. There was no way out the windows since the apartment was up several stories high. Javier locked them in the apartment when he left. He would go out and buy groceries and items they needed. He was never gone long.

Elsa learned that Javier had his way of controlling each of them. One of the women was lured into this situation because Javier started a romantic relationship with her in Mexico. He convinced her to come to the United States to be with him and start a family together. Soon after she arrived, he forced her into prostitution and then threatened to tell her parents that she was a prostitute by her own free will. Because she came from a traditional Mexican family like Elsa, she knew that the news would not only break her parent's hearts, but they would also disown her.

The other woman was there because Javier kept supplying her with crack cocaine as long as she did just as she was told. Javier had gotten her addicted as part of his plan to have her turn tricks for his financial gain. The poor woman was so addicted that she probably wouldn't have left even if Javier had left the door wide open.

Finally, Elsa found an opportunity to contact her family through Facebook to seek help. One of the Johns forgot his cell phone. Elsa hid his phone in case the John returned looking for it, but he never came back for it. At the end of the night, Elsa turned on the phone, put it on silent, and contacted her parents in Mexico. She told them that Javier had been beating her and isolating her and now she needed help getting out. She sent them the address and didn't tell them anything else. They said they would contact some friends in the United States who had moved there years ago and had now gained legal status.

About a week later, a loud knock came at the door early one morning. Javier told the women to hide because it was probably immigration coming to take them. The women believed him. Frightened, Elsa hid in her room worried that she might be detained by immigration but also relieved that this may be her way out. She heard a man's voice. The voice was inaudible at first and then she heard Javier get defensive. He was angrily cursing at the man and warning him to leave or he would get physical with him. The man got louder and Elsa could hear him threaten Javier that he would call the police to arrest him for holding a woman against her will.

Elsa could hear the defeat in Javier's voice. He settled down and told the man to take the slut with him because he didn't need her living in his apartment. He yelled for Elsa to come out. Still afraid of what would happen, Elsa came out of her bedroom. She left with a family friend who had showed up with his two sons to get Elsa. They moved Elsa in with them a few states away until she was able to financially support herself.

Elsa's Problem

Elsa was trafficked not by a stranger but by her own family member. A family member who took advantage of her vulnerability. To make matters worse, he raped her and that made her feel as if she deserved it because she moved in with a male cousin. Elsa found it difficult to escape because Javier had forced her into prostitution and had threatened to tell her parents about everything that would bring further shame and heartache.

How We Helped Elsa

Elsa came to us with hopes of obtaining legal status but also with hopes of finding a way to be able to visit her parents in her home country. It had been many years since Elsa had left home and she hadn't seen her parents since. Now, they spoke on the phone monthly, but she missed them greatly and wanted more than anything to be able to visit them.

We explained to Elsa that the T Visa leads to legal permanent residency, which allows a person to travel outside of the United States at one's leisure. The T Visa is granted for a period of four years. A year before it expires or three years after it is granted, the T Visa holder applies for legal permanent residency. However, there is also another option that allows the T Visa holder to apply for legal permanent residency after the T Visa is approved but before the three-year waiting period. Elsa found new hope and filed for the T Visa.

T Visa Summary

The T Visa is for people who have been obligated or forced to work or commit a commercial sex act. They must be forced under threat of harm or physical harm. Additionally, the applicant must not have traveled outside of the United States since escaping the trafficking.

The applicant can obtain the T Visa inside of the United States without having to exit the United States. The applicant is qualified to apply because of the harm they have suffered and because they have met the requirements of the T Visa. For this reason, there is no petitioner or sponsor involved. Proof of the trafficking is established in the applicant's written testimony.

The next step is to apply for legal permanent residency inside of the United States *without* having to exit for an interview at a consulate abroad. The residency is based on the approved T Visa so there is no petitioner or sponsor involved.

Chapter 16

Everything You Need to Know About U Visas

A PATHWAY TO CITIZENSHIP
FOR VICTIMS OF VIOLENT CRIMES

The U Visa is the most recognized of the three Humanitarian Visas. It is for people who have been victims of a crime of violence. It has a few requirements, which we will discuss in detail later. As with the T Visa, both children and adults can apply for the U Visa.

The processing time for the U Visa is the longest of all the Humanitarian Visas since more people know about it and apply for it. There is a lot of information online that has helped in spreading both awareness and education regarding the U Visa.

What does it mean to be the victim of a crime of violence?

The U Visa applicant may be the victim of any of the following crimes: abduction, abusive sexual contact, being held hostage, blackmail, domestic violence, extortion, false imprisonment, felonious assault, female genital mutilation, fraud in foreign labor contracting, incest, involuntary servitude, kidnapping, manslaughter, murder, obstruction of justice, peonage, perjury, prostitution, rape, sexual assault, sexual exploitation, slave trade, stalking, torture, trafficking, unlawful criminal restraint, witness tampering, solicitation to commit any of the named crimes, conspiracy to commit any of the named crimes, or attempt to commit any of the named crimes.

The crime must occur while the U Visa applicant is in the United States.

If any of the above crimes occurred to the person outside of the United States, they will not qualify the person for a U Visa. However, they may qualify for asylum. Asylum is a different process altogether and is very different from a Humanitarian Visa. If someone needs more information on asylum, they should consult with an attorney who focuses on asylum cases.

Who Can Obtain a U Visa?

What if the victim is an adult? If an adult, which means 21 years old or older, is the victim, then the adult may include his spouse and children as derivatives when applying for the U Visa. However, the adult victim will not be able to include parents or siblings as derivatives.

Derivatives are family members that can qualify for the same benefits as the victim. The derivatives must apply as a derivative of the Victim's application. Derivatives cannot apply for their own separate U Visa case. The derivative's family relationship to the victim is what allows the derivative to apply for the U Visa.

What if the victim is a minor child? In cases where the victim is a minor (less than 21 years old), the parents of the child can stand in the place of the minor child and cooperate with law enforcement to assist in the investigation and prosecution in the child's case.

What if the child victim is a United States citizen but has undocumented immediate family members? If the victim is under the age of 21 years old, the parents, spouse, children, and siblings (under 18 years old and unmarried) can also apply for the U Visa as derivatives. On the other hand, if the victim is 21 years old or older and is a United States citizen or permanent resident, the adult victim will not be able to apply for the U Visa. Therefore, they will not have any derivatives.

Where to Start if Applying for a U Visa

Before applying for the U Visa, the victim must obtain a signed certification from the law enforcement agency that investigated the incident. The signed certification is proof that the victim fulfilled the requirement of cooperating with the law enforcement agency in the investigation and prosecution of the case.

The first step in applying for a U Visa is not applying for the visa itself. With a U Visa, the victim must first have a *U Visa certification* that is signed by the investigating agency. This U Visa certification is proof that the victim was, is, or will be cooperative in the investigation of the crime.

The certification is a required piece of evidence in the U Visa application. Without the signed certification, the application will be rejected. Therefore, the applicant cannot skip this step of obtaining the signed certification before applying for the U Visa.

Unfortunately, the law enforcement agency has discretion as to whether they will sign the certification. At the time of the writing of this book, there are no federal laws that require the law enforcement agency to sign the certification. The agency has the discretion as to whether to sign it or not and the agency does not have to give any explanation as to why they will not sign the certification.

What if the law enforcement agency refuses to sign? If the law enforcement agency refuses to sign the certification, it means the victim cannot apply for the U Visa and cannot proceed with filing the U Visa. The opportunity for the victim to apply stops there. There is no other way around it to apply if there is no signed certification; without the certification, the application will be denied. Therefore, it is crucial to get the certification signed.

The agency may also have its own personal policy regarding which certifications they will sign. The agency may decide that they will only sign certifications for cases that are less than x years old and the agency decides what number x will be. Other agencies may decide to only sign certifications where there has been an arrest. Yet other agencies may only sign if the victim was called as a witness in a court regarding the incident. Although immigration does not require any of these factors to get the U Visa certification signed, the agency is allowed to set its own policies.

What is next after the certification is signed? Once the certification is signed, the certification is only valid six months from the date of signature. Therefore, the U Visa application must be submitted along with the signed certification prior to the six-month expiration date, which begins the date the certification was signed. If the victim fails to submit the application in that timeframe, then the certification will be considered invalid and the victim must obtain another signed certification.

After receiving the signed certification, the victim should immediately begin to work on getting their U Visa case completed and ready to submit, considering that the case can take quite some time to complete with all the work involved. The application should contain as much information as possible to show that all the requirements for the U Visa are met.

Cooperation with the Law Enforcement Agency Is Required

What does it mean to cooperate with authorities? Cooperating with authorities can be as simple as answering all of law enforcement's questions or it can be as complex as testifying in court.

Sometimes, victims make the mistake of giving the least possible information to the police because they want to report the incident but they are scared that they will get into trouble because they are undocumented. There are times when so little information is given to the police that it means they cannot do an investigation. If there is no investigation, then it will be difficult for the victim to later obtain the U Visa certification from the agency.

What if I answered all their questions but I refused to do something the law enforcement agency asked? If the victim refuses to cooperate with the law enforcement agency in any way, the agency has the discretion to refuse to sign the certification.

What if I stated that I did not want to press charges? Refusing to press charges is the same as not cooperating with the law enforcement agency, so requesting not to press charges will keep the victim from meeting the cooperation requirement. It will not make a difference if the victim is refusing to press charges in order to avoid trouble or retaliation from the aggressor.

Some victims will answer the police's questions but then notify the police that they do not want to press charges. When this happens, the reporting police officer will typically make a note in the report that the victim was no longer cooperative in the investigation. At that point, the investigation stops.

There are different things that may indicate to law enforcement that the victim no longer wishes to proceed with the investigation, other than the victim stating that they do not want to press charges. These include comments from the victim such as, "I don't want any trouble," "I want to leave things alone," "I don't know enough information about the aggressor to answer your questions," "I don't want the aggressor to get in any trouble," "The aggressor didn't mean to hurt me," "It was all a misunderstanding," "I don't speak English properly so I can't answer," "I just want to be left alone," "Everything is fine." Any of these comments can result in the officer noting in the report that the victim was uncooperative. If that happens, the victim will not be able to qualify to apply for the U Visa.

It is common for victims of domestic violence by family members or spouses to refuse to press charges. In cases between spouses, the victim may refuse to press charges because they don't want the children to lose a parent to jail or because the couple reconciles. In those situations, the victim fails to meet the cooperation requirement and the law enforcement agency will refuse to sign the certification.

Also, once the victim makes the law enforcement agency aware that he does not want to press charges, the victim cannot press charges *later*. Most cases are closed once the victim decides they do not wish to press charges. At that point, the investigation stops and so does the opportunity to press charges on the aggressor for the crime.

What if I refuse to cooperate with the law enforcement agency after my U Visa application has been submitted to immigration? Even if the U Visa application has already been submitted by the victim to immigration, the agency can contact immigration to withdraw their signed certification due to lack of cooperation. The requirement for cooperation with the law enforcement agency is not met if the victim decides to refuse to assist law enforcement. This can happen before or after the U Visa application has been submitted.

It is required that the victim applying for a U Visa cooperates with the investigation in *every* way before and after filing their application. Otherwise, the victim will fail to meet the requirements and will be denied due to not meeting the requirement of cooperating with the authorities. Most victims do not understand that they must cooperate in every way. They mistakenly believe that calling the police to report the incident, answering all the police's questions, and then refusing to press charges on the aggressor is enough to meet the requirement. However, it is not enough.

When and Why Should I Get a Copy of My Police Report?

Many victims make the huge mistake of not requesting a *copy* of the police report when the incident happens. Then, when they finally find out about the U Visa and they go to the law enforcement agency to request a copy, they discover that no police report exists. This can be a result of two factors: either the police report was never created or the agency no longer has a copy of it because so much time has lapsed.

It is essential to request a copy of the police report *as soon as possible* after the incident has occurred in order to make sure that the incident has been properly documented. Depending on the agency, the police report may still be created and the incident may still be investigated weeks after the incident occurred or this may not be the case at all. Each agency will have their own policy on this issue.

Agencies will also have their own policy on how long to *keep* their records before they are either transferred to their headquarters or discarded. Therefore, it becomes either much more difficult, or impossible, for the victim to be able to obtain a copy of their police report, thus resulting in making it difficult or impossible to obtain a signed U Visa certification.

Knowing what is *in* the report is as essential as requesting a copy of the report. Not all police reports will qualify for a U Visa. The narrative of the police report and seeing who is listed as the victim and who is listed as the aggressor is pertinent.

In domestic violence situations, it is key to know exactly what *role* the victim was given in the police report. Some victims make the mistake of assuming that because they believe they were the victims of domestic violence, they qualify for a U Visa. The police report may have the domestic charge listed as the crime investigated, but that does not automatically give the victim the role of *victim* in the report.

Many victims whose first language is not English have made the mistake of assuming they were listed as the victim in a domestic violence situation that they reported to the police. However, upon reviewing the police report, not only is the victim given the role of the aggressor, the narrative may also give a detailed description of the victim's role as the aggressor. Thus, it is impossible for the victim to apply for a U Visa based on that police report.

Although this situation may seem absurd, it is quite common in domestic violence situations. It can easily occur when the victim is the male in the situation. Even if the male victim calls the police to report the incident, the male victim may be listed as the aggressor if the female aggressor reports any harm done to her by the male victim. In other situations, male victims who could not speak English were listed as the aggressor because the English-speaking aggressor only gave their side of the story to the reporting police officer.

Frequently Asked Questions About the U Visa Certification

What if the aggressor was never arrested? The aggressor does not have to be arrested for the victim to qualify for the U Visa. In many cases, the aggressor is never arrested. Whether there is an arrest or not does not affect the case in any way. The requirement that must be met is victim cooperation with the law enforcement agency investigating the incident, not whether the cooperation led to an arrest.

What if I was not the one who called the cops? It is not required for the victim to call law enforcement. In many situations, the victim is injured and is unable to call the police. Again, as with the arrest, the importance is placed on whether the victim *cooperated* with the police in the investigation, not whether the victim called the police initially.

What if the incident happened years ago? There is no time limit as to when the incident occurred. With older cases, the focus is on being able to obtain a copy of the police report in order to request the certification from the agency. Many law enforcement agencies only keep police reports for a limited amount of time. After that time, it becomes very difficult to obtain a copy of the police report, and the agencies will usually only sign the certification if they have a copy of the original police report.

Don't Let the Requirement of Having Suffered Substantial Physical or Mental Abuse Discourage You from Applying for the U Visa

Many people are discouraged from applying for the U Visa because they don't have any medical records to prove their harm. The truth is *you don't need* any medical records because they are not required, and the harm can often be emotional only.

However, if you did require medical attention for your physical or emotional harm, then it is best to provide the medical documents with your application. If your harm was emotional, you do not have to provide any medical records as proof.

What is emotional harm? Emotional harm can manifest in many different forms. Every person is different. After the incident, some people may suffer from anxiety and nightmares. Others may be traumatized to the point that they fear leaving their home. In cases where a gun was involved and was shot, the victim may continue to fear the sound of loud noises. In cases where the victim was assaulted by a person of a specific race or gender, the victim may fear being around people of that race or gender.

So, how do you prove that you meet the substantial harm requirement without medical records? The answer is quite simple. You prove your substantial harm by explaining in writing how you were harmed in a personal declaration that is signed by you. Your signature attests that all that is written is true.

How Long Will It Take to Get a Decision on My U Visa Case?

U Visa case processing times have continued to increase since the U Visa became increasingly popular starting in 2013. By 2013, many victims had discovered the U Visa and started to apply because there is no limit regarding how long ago the problem occurred. Therefore, many victims with older police reports started to seek out immigration attorneys to help them apply for the U Visa. Other people who had not yet been victims of a crime became aware that if they ever were the victim of a crime, they should immediately report the crime to police because it would be the only way to help them apply to obtain legal status in the United States.

After the U Visa gained popularity, there started to be more applications than there were U Visas available each year. Every year there are only 10,000 U Visas available. However, there are well over 10,000 U Visa applications submitted each year. According to the United States Citizenship and Immigration Services, in 2016, 60,710 U Visa applications were submitted. Thus, the processing times extend longer and longer every year.

United States Department of Homeland Security. *Number of Service-wide Forms by Fiscal Year-to-Date, Quarter, and Form Status 2015 Number of Service-wide Forms by Fiscal Year-to-Date, Quarter, and Form Status 2016.* http://www.ilw.com/immigrationdaily/news/2016,1228-USCISAllForms.pdf.

Chapter 17

Patricio's Story

HOW AN UNDOCUMENTED MAN OBTAINED A U VISA
BECAUSE HE WAS FELONIOUSLY ASSAULTED

Patricio came to the United States over a decade ago. He was hardworking and lived with his wife and two kids. He'd always gone to church regularly with his family, and they stayed busy with their church family.

One day, he came home after work to find that some new neighbors were moving in across the street. There were five men moving in with no families, and Patricio went over to greet them.

Patricio asked if they needed any help. He told them where he lived and told them to let him know if they needed anything. Patricio let them know that he was happy they moved in because there weren't any other Hispanic males living in the neighborhood.

Patricio's wife Esther was a stay-at-home mom. She was home most of the day alone while the children were at school and Patricio was at work. Esther hadn't seen or met their new neighbors. She knew they were single men living without families so she thought it inappropriate to go over to meet them.

A couple days after the neighbors moved in, Esther had her first awkward encounter with them. A couple of the men were sitting on their front porch when she arrived home after grocery shopping. The men were sitting there drinking beer. They saw her and started to whistle and call out to her. She ignored them and didn't give in to their advances. Esther quickly grabbed the groceries and went inside the house. By the time that Patricio had gotten home from work, Esther was so preoccupied with cooking dinner, the kid's homework, and getting them ready for bed that she forgot to mention the incident to Patricio.

That weekend, as Patricio and the family were arriving home, all the men were sitting on their porch drinking. Patricio waved to them and went inside with his family. He figured if they were drinking he shouldn't go over because they would probably want him to drink a beer with them. Esther remembered the incident that happened just days earlier. She figured she shouldn't say anything to Patricio since it was probably a misunderstanding and the men hadn't realized she was Patricio's wife.

A couple days later, Esther was home alone. She went out to run errands and arrived back home around noon. Immediately, she noted that two men were sitting on their porch drinking beer. She hesitated before exiting her car. Again, the men started whistling at her. However, this time they made inappropriate comments to her about her body. Esther knew she would have to tell Patricio about this incident when he got home.

Esther went inside the house and locked the door. She felt safe. A few minutes later, there was a knock on the door. She didn't have to ask who it was because she heard the man outside making comments. She could tell that he was heavily intoxicated by the way he was slurring his speech. Esther was afraid and didn't know what to do. If she called the police, they could question her about her immigration status and she could get herself and Patricio in trouble if they found out that they were undocumented. Esther threatened the man with calling the police. Thankfully, that was enough to make him go away.

That evening, when Patricio got home from work Esther told him what happened. She was still shaken by the incident. Patricio knew he had to put a stop to this behavior.

When Patricio walked across the street to the neighbor's house, there were now three men on the porch drinking. Patricio walked up to them calmly and asked which one of them had come over to his house to bother his wife. None of the men admitted to it. One of them made derogatory comments claiming that none of them cared for his wife. Then, he threatened Patricio, telling him to leave if he didn't want to get hurt for falsely accusing them of disturbing his wife. Patricio told them that he didn't want any trouble and simply asked that they leave his wife alone. He told them it was disrespectful.

As Patricio walked back to his house he heard a yell behind him and turned around. He turned just in time to brace himself for the impact of one of the men who charged at him. It startled Patricio, and all he could do was put his hands up to block the hit. Suddenly, Patricio was on the ground, and the man had a knife to his neck. Patricio fought back and managed to push the man away from him. The man yelled at Patricio, warning him that he shouldn't have messed with them. Then, the man turned around and went home.

Patricio lay there watching as the man returned to his house. He was too shaken up and scared to do anything else. He didn't even call 911, even though the phone was in his pocket the entire time.

However, Esther had seen the entire incident and called 911 for help. Once the police arrived, they went to Patricio's home and asked him what had happened. Patricio explained the entire situation as he knew it to the police officer. Patricio allowed the police officer to take pictures of the cut that the man left on Patricio's neck from the attack. Then, Patricio walked with the police officer across the street to identify the man that attacked him. No one answered the door.

The police officer left after taking down the information and attempting to speak to someone at the neighbor's house. The officer asked Patricio if he needed to be taken to the hospital. Patricio said he was fine and an ambulance wasn't necessary. Patricio was thankful that he had not been stabbed or injured. He'd received a minor cut on his neck, but it would heal quickly.

That night, Patricio and Esther couldn't sleep. They were up all night fearful that the men would return to attack them while they were sleeping and hurt them and the children. They had called the police, but the attacker was not arrested. They feared he would come to seek revenge for calling the cops on him.

The next day, Patricio didn't see any sign of the men. He hoped that calling the police scared them enough to keep them away. Then, another day passed, and there was still no sign of them. A week later and nothing. Another neighbor told Patricio that the men had left in the middle of the night a few days after the incident. That was the last time Patricio or any of the neighbors ever saw them.

The police officer that had arrived on the scene called Patricio a couple of days in a row after the incident. The police officer was following up to see if Patricio had any other information about the man that attacked him. Patricio told him that he hadn't seen them.

After the attack, Patricio and Esther lived with constant fear and anxiety. They hadn't slept well in months. Patricio installed an alarm in his home, and he bought a gun for protection. They didn't let the children play outside unsupervised, and they made sure to always keep their doors bolted.

Patricio's Problem

Patricio and Esther came to us distressed and exhausted. They'd been suffering for years after the attack. They were tired of not being able to overcome the fear and anxiety they constantly felt. Before the attack, they were a happy family. They went to church regularly and attended community functions. They had many close friends at church and were very social with them. Now, they were different people. The attack had changed them, and they still had not been able to get back to being who they once were. Their marriage was suffering, and they missed the couple they had been.

It was only recently that a close friend saw one of our videos online regarding the U Visa and told Patricio about the option. He knew what

Patricio had suffered and knew that he and Esther still suffered because of the incident. Patricio's friend encouraged him to find out more and to look at the opportunity to obtain a U Visa as a way of obtaining justice for the parts of their lives that were taken from their family and their marriage.

Patricio sought us out because he believed that part of the reason they had not gotten over the attack was because the attacker had never been arrested. The attacker just moved away and never returned. He was still out there and could attack Patricio again or hurt someone else.

How We Helped Patricio

One thing we can do for sure is help victims apply for the visas they qualify for, and that is exactly how we helped Patricio and Esther. After listening to Patricio's story, reviewing his police report, and asking him a few questions, we knew that he qualified for the U Visa.

Like many victims, Patricio did not go to get a copy of his police report until he found out about the U Visa several years after the incident. Patricio wanted the copy so he could find out from an attorney if he qualified for the U Visa. Fortunately, the agency did have a copy of the police report and they gave it to him.

Patricio's biggest concern was that he wouldn't be able to prove that he was substantially harmed because he wasn't stabbed by his attacker. Furthermore, he didn't seek medical attention the day of the attack.

We explained to Patricio that medical records are not required to apply for the U Visa. We let him know that his proof of harm would be to document and explain how he was both physically and emotionally harmed by the attack in a personal declaration. Patricio felt much more comfortable knowing that signing the personal declaration would be his proof that he was telling the truth about the substantial harm he suffered because of the attack.

What Could Have Gone Wrong and Disqualified Patricio as a U Visa Victim

Like Patricio, the first mistake that many victims make is that they do not call the police for help. In this case, his wife saw that he was being attacked and decided to call the police. However, Patricio did not call the police himself. It is common for victims not to call the police when they are in a dangerous situation.

Victims know that they need help, but they are more concerned with what will happen to them if they call the police and the police find out that they are undocumented. Their fear is that calling the police will result in their deportation, so many victims will never contact the police about the incident that occurred. Some will want to report the incident once they know that it could help them apply for a U Visa, but by that time too much time has passed for the police to do an investigation on the incident. If an extended amount of time has lapsed since the incident, the police will typically just do an informational report, which does not lead to an investigation as is required for the U Visa.

Another mistake that victims make is that they do not cooperate with the authorities in the investigation. The victims may refuse to answer any questions from the police because they want to keep the police from asking about their immigration status. Other victims are afraid to answer any questions because they do not want the aggressor to retaliate. The victim fears that if they report the aggressor to the police, the aggressor will then retaliate by reporting the undocumented individual to immigration.

However, in this case, Patricio had spoken to the police when they arrived, even though he was not the one who called them. He not only answered all their questions but he explained to the police officer everything that happened. This helped the police to create a police report for the investigation. Patricio completely cooperated with the authorities, not only after the attack but also over the two days when the police officer called to follow up with him.

WHAT HAPPENS AFTER I APPLY FOR THE U VISA?

✓ 30 DAYS AFTER SUBMITTING YOUR APPLICATION TO IMMIGRATION, **YOU WILL RECEIVE A RECEIPT INDICATING THAT YOUR CASE IS PENDING.**

✓ 60 DAYS AFTER SUBMITTING YOUR APPLICATION TO IMMIGRATION, **YOU WILL RECEIVE YOUR BIOMETRICS APPOINTMENT.**

✓ YOUR CASE WILL BE PROCESSED ACCORDING TO THE PROCESSING TIMES LISTED ON THE USCIS.GOV WEBSITE, **THEN YOU WILL RECEIVE A DECISION ON YOUR CASE.**

Processing times are approximate.

HONEST IMMIGRATION.

www.honestimmigration.com

Chapter 18

Emilia's Story

When Emilia was just 12 years old, she had to drop out of school because her parents couldn't afford to pay for her education anymore. She had three younger siblings for whom her parents had to pay school tuition. Emilia figured she would probably meet the same fate that her older sister did when she was 13 years old. In a desperate financial situation, her parents allowed an older man to pay them in exchange for marrying their daughter. Her husband moved away with her, and Emilia hadn't seen or heard of her since.

Arranged Marriage

It wasn't long before Emilia's father put her on display for men to see. He would have her mother clean her up and put on her nicest dress. They would come over and look at her. They didn't ask her anything. They just stared at her then privately spoke with her father. She could tell by the defeated look on her mother's face that she, too, would be sold to the highest bidder.

Emilia was afraid, but she knew that her younger siblings would benefit from the money. They barely had enough to eat. Her dad couldn't find work. Emilia couldn't help but wonder if that had anything to do with him always being drunk.

After a few short weeks, Emilia knew that her father had found a husband for her. That day, her mother couldn't stop crying. She hid her face, but Emilia knew she was sad. She told Emilia to be strong and that she loved her. Emilia only wished her dad would have done the same.

That evening, a man came to the house. He didn't even come inside. Her father had her ready at the door and handed her over just as quickly as the man had knocked on the door. Emilia knew crying wouldn't make a difference. She knew that trying to run away would only make things worse for her. After all, it's not like the man was kidnapping her. Her parents were giving her to him.

His name was Axel, and he was 29 years old.

Axel made arrangements the next day to have Emilia crossed into the United States. He told her that he would meet her on the other side. He said she should listen to the woman who would take her across the border.

Child Molestation and Pregnancy

Emilia would have never imagined the situation she would be living in. Axel was already married and they had three small children. Emilia was purchased to be his maid and help take care of their children so Axel could put his wife to work cleaning houses.

Right away, Axel laid down the rules prohibiting Emilia and the wife to speak to each other. Emilia was to take orders only from him.

After work, Axel drank excessively and was abusive toward his wife, Emilia and the children. It wasn't long before Axel started to go into Emilia's bedroom at night to rape her. He told her that she was like his second wife. Emilia didn't know whether the wife knew this was going on or not. If the wife knew, she never let on. The woman looked exhausted all the time. Emilia couldn't ask her for help because Axel was always there when the wife was home.

A couple of years later, Emilia became pregnant. She was only 14 years old. She was scared by the changes going on with her body. She didn't even know she was pregnant until Axel became angry with her and told her she was going to have a baby. She hadn't been feeling well for a few days. Axel saw her in the restroom vomiting one morning and he became furious. He told her not to think that she was going to get out of doing her chores around the house. Even while pregnant, Emilia had to do the housecleaning, cook breakfast, do the laundry, and help with the children.

Emilia was scared. She hadn't spoken to her parents since Axel took her from her home. There were changes going on with her body that made her feel awful most days. She wished she could speak to her mother and ask her what to do. Emilia knew that now she could never expect to return home.

Abandoned at the Hospital

Nine months later, Emilia woke up in terrible pain. The pain was unbearable every time her stomach contracted. She went to the restroom thinking that she might throw up.

As she lay on the restroom floor, Axel walked in and saw her. He kicked her leg and told her to get up and get dressed. Emilia thought he might actually take her to see a doctor. She managed to get up and get dressed hoping that he would find her a doctor.

Axel told her to get in the car. She didn't ask any questions because she knew he was already angry. They drove to a hospital, where he stopped the car before reaching the entrance. He told her that she better not mention his name or any of his family members. Axel told her that if anyone asked her age, she should say that she was eighteen years old. He threatened that if she didn't obey, he would see to it that her parents and siblings in Mexico were killed.

He told her to get out of the car and walk to the entrance. Emilia obeyed. Struggling and in agonizing pain, she walked into the hospital. A nurse in the emergency room saw her. Emilia couldn't speak English so she had no way of communicating with the nurse. But the nurse knew that Emilia was in labor.

Emilia delivered a baby boy that night. Yet the peace and alone time she was enjoying with her baby was short-lived. The next morning, a social worker came to speak with Emilia. She spoke Spanish and started asking Emilia lots of questions. Emilia remembered what Axel told her. She told the woman that she was 18 years old. She lied and said she had come alone to the United States and that she didn't have any identifying documents.

The social worker knew that Emilia wasn't telling her the entire truth regarding her living situation but wanted to help her now that she had a baby. She told Emilia that if she told the truth about what happened, she could help her find a place where she would be safe. Emilia thought about her newborn son, the fact that she had nowhere to go, and no one to keep Axel from hurting her. She told the social worker the truth about what happened. The police were called in to take a report and investigate the situation. The social worker helped Emilia into a shelter for battered women.

Axel was never arrested since the house was found abandoned when the police went searching for him.

Emilia's Problem

Even though it's been years since Emilia was abandoned at the hospital, she still fears that Axel will come looking for her in retaliation for reporting him to the police. She doesn't know if he abandoned the home because he knew she reported him or if he left in case she reported him.

Once the shelter helped her to get on her feet, she moved to a different state. Now, she is married and has two more children. However, she still struggles daily from the abuse she suffered as a child.

How We Helped Emilia

Emilia is now focused on her family and moving forward for their sake. She found out from a friend that a U Visa could be an option for her and her husband to gain legal status so she made an appointment and both of them came to our office for information.

They wanted to be able to get a driver's license so they could drive without fear of being arrested. They wanted to get a better job to support their children but they needed work permits to do that. They also wanted to feel secure and not have to fear being deported.

We discussed her situation and discovered she met the requirements for both the U Visa and T Visa. She met the requirements for the U Visa because she reported the abuse to law enforcement. She also met the requirements for the T Visa because she was the victim of human trafficking.

Both of these humanitarian visas provide a driver's license and work permit. These are the options Emilia has that will help her have the future she and her husband desire. It will be up to Emilia to decide if she wants to pursue one or both Visas. The main difference between the two visas is the processing times. At the time that Emilia consulted with us, the U Visa had a five year wait and the T Visa had a one year wait.

Emilia's biggest concern was whether applying for a humanitarian visa would require Axel's involvement in any way. She lived in hiding from him and didn't want him to know anything about their whereabouts. We explained to Emilia that the U Visa and T Visa were designed to protect the victim. This included keeping their address and information confidential. At no point in time would immigration contact Axel and let him know anything about her application. Emilia was relieved and hopeful when she heard this.

Chapter 19

Cristobal's Story

One afternoon, Cristobal received a call from his wife, Rachel, while he was at work. She normally didn't call him at work because she knew that Cristobal's work had a strict policy of limited personal cell phone use. The first time she called, he let it ring until it went to his voice mail. A few seconds later, she called again. Cristobal knew to answer since she was calling twice in a row. When Cristobal answered her call, never had he imagined what he would hear. Her scream pierced his eardrum. Something was terribly wrong.

At first, Cristobal couldn't make out what she was saying. Then, slowly, as he made out some of the words through her uncontrollable sobs, he realized she was telling him that their son, Andrew, had been shot and he was gone. As his heart raced, Cristobal could only respond by asking her where she was. She told him she was at the hospital. He said he would be right there. Cristobal left his work after briefly telling a friend to let their supervisor know he had a family emergency.

On the drive home, a million different questions raced through his mind. Who had shot their son? Why was he shot? Where was he when he was shot? Their son was only eight years old; how could someone not have stopped this from happening? And where could he have gone to—certainly he wasn't dead?

When Cristobal arrived at the hospital, several family members were there with Rachel, comforting her and mourning their loss. Rachel fell into Cristobal's arms sobbing uncontrollably. All she could say was, "Our baby is gone."

As they sat in the hospital lobby, Cristobal slowly heard the story, from his family, regarding what had happened. Andrew had arrived home from school on the bus with his older brother and his younger sister. Rachel, who was a stay-at-home mom, greeted the children when they got home. As usual, the children went outside to play before dinner, and Rachel watched them through the window as she started cooking.

Andrew came in and asked Rachel if he could go over to his neighbor's house to play. Since his friend lived only a couple of houses down the street, Rachel allowed him to go.

About an hour later, Rachel heard a loud sound. It sounded like someone had set off a firework. Moments later, her older son ran into the house telling her that he had heard a gunshot. Rachel looked around and saw that her daughter was watching TV, but Andrew still hadn't returned from the neighbor's house. She told her older son to go find Andrew and tell him to come home. She didn't want her children outside if someone was shooting off a gun.

About five minutes later, she heard her older son outside screaming for her. She looked out the window and saw that he was crying and looked very pale. He was running from the direction of where Andrew's friend lived. Rachel ran outside and before she could ask him what was wrong, he told her that Andrew had been shot and he was bleeding badly. Rachel was shocked and she followed her son to the neighbor's house.

The front door of the house was still open. As they ran inside, they didn't see any adults inside the home. Andrew was lying on the floor, face down, in the doorway of one of the bedrooms. He was alone, and his blood was soaking the carpet beneath him. Rachel embraced Andrew and told her son to run home to get her cell phone. When he returned, she called 911. Since she couldn't speak English, she had her son tell the operator that his brother had been shot and they needed an ambulance right away. A couple of hours later, Andrew was pronounced dead at the hospital.

The family later found out that Andrew had gone over to his 10-year-old neighbor's house when the boy's parents were not at home. Another boy around their age had joined them to play. The neighbor showed them his father's gun. He then loaded the gun as he had seen his father do and pretended to shoot his friends. Andrew got scared when his neighbor cocked the gun. When Andrew got up to leave, the neighbor demanded that he not leave. He was afraid that Andrew would tell on him and get him in trouble. When Andrew refused to stay, the neighbor boy fired the gun at Andrew.

Cristobal and Rachel spent the next several weeks going down to the police station and answering all the police department's questions about Andrew's murder. They drove their older son down to the department several times because he had been one of the first to arrive on the scene after Andrew was shot. Furthermore, they all attended and served as witnesses during the court trials.

Cristobal's Problem

Cristobal and Rachel had lived mourning their son's death for years. They were undocumented and so was their older son, whom they had brought to the United States when he was a baby. Aside from having to live with the daily pain of losing a son, they also lived with the fear of being deported. They had already suffered so much from losing their younger son and they didn't want to be separated from their other two children because of deportation. They also feared what would happen to their son if he was detained and separated from them. They knew that if they were deported, crossing the border undocumented to return to the United States could be a fatal undertaking.

How We Helped Cristobal

Cristobal came to us after there was an immigration raid in their town and several people they knew had been detained. Reality set in and they realized that it could easily have been them who were detained and separated from their children. They feared there would be another raid soon, and they were desperate to find a way to stay in the United States legally.

They contacted us wanting to find out about a law someone had mentioned that gave people residency automatically if they had been in the country for more than 10 years. After reassuring Cristobal that no such law existed, I explained to Cristobal that they had an option to apply for the U Visa as indirect victims because their child had been the victim of a crime of violence.

Cristobal's biggest concerns were that they would not qualify for the U Visa because they were not the victims of the crime and their son, Andrew, had been a United States citizen. They thought that they needed to be listed as victims on the police report and that the child victim had to be undocumented. I explained to them that under the U Visa, parents who are undocumented can apply as indirect victims if the child is the victim of a crime in the United States, so long as the parents either assisted law enforcement by having the child available to cooperate in the investigation of the crime or the parents themselves cooperated in the investigation of the crime.

Furthermore, I explained that the child had to be under 21 years of age and that the child's immigration status was not relevant. It did not matter whether the child was undocumented or had some legal immigration status. For the parents to qualify as indirect victims, they had to possess information about the crime and they had to have been helpful to law enforcement in the investigation or prosecution of the crime.

For the parents to possess information that would qualify them as indirect victims required that the parents had credible and reliable information about the crime activity. The parents must have detailed information about the crime or have information about the events leading up to the crime, and the information should assist the law enforcement agency in the investigation or prosecution of the crime.

Once they understood how the U Visa allowed them as parents to apply for the U Visa, they asked how they could help their older son obtain legal status. I explained that the U Visa allows an adult who is applying to include their undocumented spouse and their undocumented children that are under 21 years old and unmarried to be included as derivatives in the application. The derivatives obtain the U Visa just like the applicant does. The applicant should apply and include their spouse and children as derivatives so they can all obtain the U Visa. Therefore, in this case, Cristobal would be applying as the principal and he would include Rachel and their son as derivatives.

U Visa Summary

The U Visa is for victims of a crime of violence within the United States. The victim must have cooperated with law enforcement in investigating or prosecuting the criminal activity. Additionally, the victim must have suffered mentally or physically.

The U Visa can be applied for either inside or outside of the United States. For victims applying for the U Visa within the United States, they do not have to exit the United States to obtain the visa. For victims applying for the U Visa outside of the United States, they will remain abroad until their visa is approved. At that point, the U Visa can be picked up at the United States consulate in the country where they are residing and they can enter the United States.

The next step is to apply for legal permanent residency based on the approved U Visa. This does not require a petitioner or a sponsor. Until now, no interview has been required to obtain residency via the U Visa.

The Conclusion

You were brought to the United States unfairly or were mistreated after you arrived. You have rights to protect you from the dangers that immigrants face after they escape their tormentors. You shouldn't and don't have to live in fear and hiding from your tormentor. There is a way to seek justice. It may not mean putting your tormentor behind bars, but it means you can gain legal status to right the wrong you have suffered.

United States Citizenship and Immigration Services has a variety of different visas and programs to help people that need aid due to coercion, abuse, and other urgent circumstances that they have been subjected to. Each option has its own set of requirements that must be met so one can qualify to apply. These requirements protect against any abuse of a system that provides opportunities to help those who are in true need of assistance.

Never assume that gaining legal status is as easy as filling out forms. Every immigration law is complex. You should be working with an attorney on your immigration case. Getting help from a non-attorney to submit your paperwork could result in mistakes that could cost you your freedom. Also, seek legal advice *only* from an attorney who is licensed to practice law in the United States.

It would be an honor to help you. Contact us at honestimmigration.com.

Frequently Asked Questions Regarding VAWA, U Visa, and T Visa

What proof do I need to show that the incident happened?

Other than the U Visa, which requires a signed U Visa certification, the only proof that is required to submit with your application is your signed testimony. Your testimony should describe the details regarding the incident and the harm you suffered.

What if my incident happened many years ago—can I still apply?

Yes. There is no time limit as to when the incident occurred.

What happens if my case is denied?

If your case is denied, you should file a motion or an appeal. Filing a motion or an appeal will prevent the decision from becoming final and will likely help in preventing you from being placed in removal proceedings.

Will I have to attend an interview with immigration?

No. There is no interview when applying for VAWA, T Visa, or U Visa. However, there may be an interview within the United States when applying for residency based on the approved visa.

Am I putting myself at risk of deportation by applying for a Humanitarian Visa?

Living in the United States *undocumented* puts an individual at risk daily of being detained by immigration and likely being deported. Although applying for a Humanitarian Visa does not prevent a person from being detained, it can help tremendously in preventing a person being deported if they can go ahead and complete the application process.

What if I don't have a police report regarding the incident?

Police reports are not required for VAWA, U Visas, or T Visas.

If I apply for a Humanitarian Visa, will immigration have my address and know how to find me?

No. It is not necessary to include your address on your Humanitarian Visa application. Instead, you can use your attorney's address or get permission to use another address.

Does immigration expect me to know my trafficker's name or the address where I was trafficked?

No. Victims are not expected to know the names of their traffickers or the addresses where they were trafficked.

If the Humanitarian Visas have been around for so long, how did I not know about them?

Despite how long these Humanitarian Visas have been around, there is still a need for more education regarding these options. Also, not all immigration attorneys take these types of cases.

Is going to a Notario the same as going to an attorney?

No. A Notario does not have a license to practice law in the United States. Most importantly, Notarios are not held responsible for their mistakes on cases.

After my visa is approved, will I need to leave the country to apply for residency?

No. Applying for residency based on an approved VAWA, T Visa, or U Visa is done *inside* the United States.

I qualify for a Humanitarian Visa, but is there a better way to gain legal status?

Not unless you can find another option that will allow you to gain legal status and then obtain residency within the United States even when you don't have anyone to petition for you or sponsor you. And let's not forget to mention the ability to include your spouse, children, and potentially other family members as derivatives.

If I filed for asylum, can I still apply for a Humanitarian Visa?

Yes. Because of the low asylum approval rates, anyone applying for asylum should seek other options as potential backups in the event that their asylum case is denied.

Does the public charge affect me?

No. By law, the public charge cannot affect VAWA, T Visa, and U Visa applicants. Nor does it affect the applicant obtaining Residency based on an approved VAWA, T Visa, or U Visa.

Can I still apply if I have multiple undocumented entries and a deportation?

Yes. Generally, having multiple undocumented entries, a deportation, or a deportation order will not prevent a person from being able to apply.

Does an attorney need to go with me to the biometrics fingerprint appointment?

No. You can go alone to the fingerprint appointment. At the appointment, you will turn in your appointment notice upon arrival. Then, your name will be called. Next, you will have your fingerprints and photo taken. This will usually take less than 10 minutes. Afterwards, you are free to leave.

Do I get a work permit or a driver's license while I wait?

No. There is no work permit or driver's license offered while your case is pending. However, if you are placed on a waiting list prior to your case being approved, you may have deferred action granted. Deferred action will allow you a work permit, driver's license, and social security number.

Who can I add as a derivative?

Usually, adults that are 21 years old and older can apply for a spouse and children under 21 years old that are single. If the applicant is under 21 years old, he may be able to also include siblings and parents.

Once my visa is approved, can I travel outside the United States?

Traveling on a visa requires permission to travel. Permission can be sought by requesting Advance Parole. However, typically, we do not recommend traveling outside of the United States until you have been granted *legal permanent residency*, which does not require you to request permission to travel.

What does the Humanitarian Visa give me if it is granted?

Having a Humanitarian Visa granted gives you a work permit, permission to obtain a driver's license, and a social security number.

www.ingramcontent.com/pod-product-compliance
Lightning Source LLC
Chambersburg PA
CBHW070935030426
42336CB00014BA/2690